HOW DID WE GET HERE?

ALSO BY ROBERT DALLEK

HOW DID WE GET HERE?

FROM THEODORE ROOSEVELT
TO DONALD TRUMP

ROBERT DALLEK

HARPER PERENNIAL

NEW YORK • LONDON • TORONTO • SYDNEY • NEW DELHI • AUCKLAND

HARPER ● PERENNIAL

A hardcover edition of this book was published in 2020 by HarperCollins Publishers.

HarperCollins books may be purchased for educational, business, or sales promotional use. For information, please email the Special Markets Department at SPsales@harpercollins.com.

FIRST HARPER PERENNIAL EDITION PUBLISHED 2021.

Library of Congress Cataloging-in-Publication Data has been applied for.

ISBN 978-0-06-287300-2 (pbk.)

21 22 23 24 25   LSC   10 9 8 7 6 5 4 3 2 1

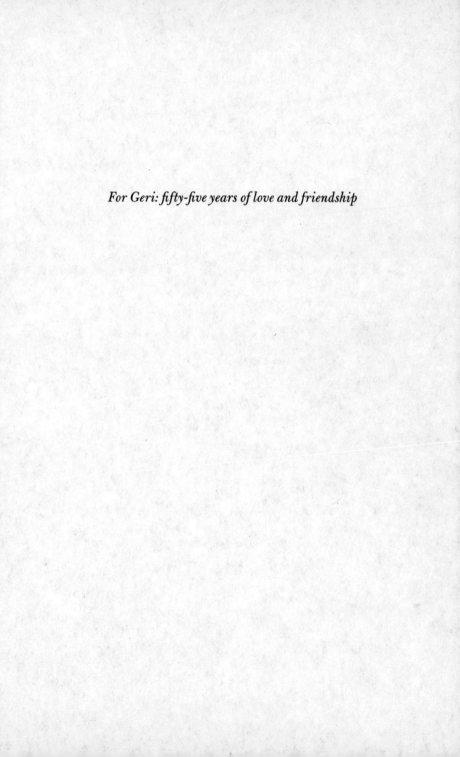

For Geri: fifty-five years of love and friendship

In easy times history is more or less of an ornamental art,
but in times of danger we are driven to the written record
by a pressing need to find answers to the riddles of today.
We need to know what kind of firm ground other men,
belonging to generations before us, have found to stand on.

—JOHN DOS PASSOS, 1941[1]

Contents

HOW DID WE GET HERE?

Introduction

At the conclusion of the Constitutional Convention in September 1787, a Philadelphia citizen asked Benjamin Franklin, "What sort of government have you given us?" Franklin famously replied, "A Republic, if you can keep it."

The struggle to preserve the Republic has never been easy or without perils. The rise of political parties, which the founders opposed; the conflict between Federalists and Democratic-Republicans over how to respond to European turmoil from the wars of the French Revolution; and President John Adams's Alien and Sedition Acts repressing the press and free speech made Franklin's conditional response seem all too prophetic. The 1800 election in which Thomas Jefferson was denounced as the antichrist and Adams was described as a hermaphrodite—half-man, half-woman—moved Jefferson to decry partisanship in his 1801 Inaugural Address and defend the first peaceful transfer of political power from one party to another by saying, "We are all Federalists; We are all Republicans; We are all . . . Americans."[1] The Civil War of 1861–65 was the greatest assault on the Republic's ability to work out political differences peacefully.

But new perils lay ahead. Industrial strife, economic downturns or "panics," and corruption plagued late nineteenth-century American politics. Henry Adams, the offspring of the great Adams family, argued in 1919's *The Degradation of the Democratic Dogma* that America's democracy inevitably would collapse. The Teapot Dome scandal of the Warren G. Harding administration; the failure of Herbert Hoover to address effectively the economic depression of the 1930s; the disputes over foreign policy preceding World War II, including the battle to combat the anti-war isolationists preaching America First; postwar recriminations about communism at home and abroad; Joseph McCarthy's ruthless invective in denouncing political opponents in the 1950s; the misguided commitment to the Vietnam War in the 1960s; the Watergate scandal in the 1970s that forced the only presidential resignation in history; the George W. Bush war in Iraq that never revealed weapons of mass destruction; and now the Trump administration that remains under investigation for corruption, and for welcoming Russian interference in the 2016 election, and for pressing Ukraine to investigate and denounce Joe Biden and his son, were evidence enough to impeach Trump and provide enduring support for Henry Adams's forecast.

These strains gave additional appeal to demagogues using mass media, through which populist leaders thrived. Their pronouncements on easy fixes to economic and social problems at home and shifting dangers abroad made them attractive figures to millions of people.

In 1959, the journalist Richard Rovere declared, "We have been, by and large, lucky [in having few national demagogues but] there is no assurance our luck will hold. . . . For a nation that has known a good deal of mob rule and that—in its devotion to public liberties— makes mobs quite easily accessible to demagogues, we have had, I think, remarkable good fortune in having had so little trouble."[2] The rise of the penny press, or widely available daily newspapers promoting provocative, scandal-mongering "yellow journalism," followed by the introduction of radio, television, and now social media, where tweets can instantly reach millions of Americans, has lent appeal to unscrupulous politicians seeking high office. As the historian Richard Hofstadter explained in 1948, because "the ideology of self-help, free enterprise, and beneficent cupidity upon which Americans have been nourished" has faded, "Americans have become more receptive than ever to dynamic personal leadership as a substitute."[3]

The country's attraction during the 1930s depression to Louisiana's Huey Long, whom Franklin Roosevelt called one of the two most dangerous men in America (along with General Douglas MacArthur), and the subsequent affinity for Wisconsin senator Joseph McCarthy's anti-communist crusade that recklessly victimized innocent Americans, gave Rovere reason to think that our luck was running out.

The resistance to putting a demagogue in the White House held up during the anti-communist agitation of the 1950s and the Vietnam War in the 1960s. But Vietnam opened the way to Richard Nixon's election in 1968, and Watergate once again tested the viability of our democratic institutions and the rule of law. Nixon's resignation in August 1974 moved Vice President Gerald Ford, his successor, to declare, "My fellow Americans, our long national nightmare is over."[4]

But was it? Donald Trump's 2016 election to the White House has presented a new challenge to our system of government. His lying about a host of things (over ten thousand lies, according to the *Washington Post*) has undermined his credibility and further weakened public faith in government or, more precisely, the way we govern ourselves. We are now in the fourth year of the Trump presidency and in the midst of another, perhaps more formidable, challenge to traditional republican institutions. And while it is still too soon to tell how this part of the story will turn out, or what the full impact of his administration will be on the American system of government at home and its relations with allies and adversaries abroad, it is already clear that this is not a conventional administration with a traditional chief executive mindful of constructive presidential actions, or respectful of the rule of law and the men and women who enforce it. As twenty-seven mental health experts argued in *The Dangerous Case of Donald Trump*, he is a deeply insecure man who needs to counter his sense of limits with a grandiosity that alleges his superiority in wealth and accomplishment to everyone. It is a troubling assertion of a false reality that threatens the national well-being.

What in our past politics and presidential administrations opened the way to this current assault on American democracy? And more important, what in our earlier history allowed us to create a reasonably well functioning system of governance that echoed Franklin Roosevelt's assertion, "Better the occasional faults of a Government that lives in a spirit of charity than the consistent omissions of a Government frozen in the ice of its own indifference."[5]

It is the Theodore Roosevelt, Woodrow Wilson, Franklin Roosevelt, Harry Truman, Dwight Eisenhower, John Kennedy, Lyndon Johnson, Richard Nixon, Jimmy Carter, and Ronald Reagan presidencies discussed in this book that have advanced both the national well-being and the turn toward the troublesome Trump administration. To Trump, unaware of their histories, all these administrations were pretty much a blank slate. It was only with the George W. Bush, Bill Clinton, and Barack Obama presidencies that he saw vulnerabilities he thought he could exploit to become president. Yet there were traditions in place that made Trump's ascent to the presidency and behavior in office possible. While each of these pre-Trump governments had distinctive qualities that separated them from their predecessors and successors, they shared defects that made them all, to one degree or other, architects of our present hopes and dilemmas. Some were certainly more complicit than others in giving rise to current events, but they are all worth considering as designers of present-day concerns.

None of this is meant to suggest that I will offer any exhaustive treatment of these modern presidential administrations. My focus is on aspects of these presidencies that served as preludes to Donald Trump. The George W. Bush, Bill Clinton, and Barack Obama administrations are of obvious significance, too, in bringing Trump to the fore, but I feel these administrations are too recent to be fully open to convincing historical judgment. As a historian schooled in taking the longer view of events, I will largely confine this book to the administrations from Roosevelt to Reagan.

Lest I seem intent strictly on the underside of these presidencies, I intend to underscore the effectiveness of these presidents as well, and to inject a measure of hope into the current national malaise about politics. Our most successful presidents offered a realizable vision, used their understanding of politics and personal popularity to get there, built a national consensus to achieve their goals, and were mindful that their credibility was essential to their effectiveness. How Trump measures up to these standards is one way to think about his performance as president. In brief, these earlier administrations partly tell us how we got here. But they also underscore how different the Trump presidency is from what came before.

In 1941, the novelist John Dos Passos wrote in *The Ground We Stand On*, "In times of change and danger when there is a quicksand of fear under men's reasoning, a sense of continuity with generations gone before can stretch like a lifeline across the scary present."

In this age of Trump, our history can provide some reassurance that we will restore our better angels to the councils of government.

But we do well also to recall how earlier administrations and public outlook facilitated the rise of so unpresidential a character as Donald Trump to the White House and, at the same time, how different he and his administration are from past presidents and presidencies. I would like to think of this book as a cautionary tale reminding us that the only constant in history is change, but whether for good or ill is the choice we can make. It is no small irony, then, that after the Trump presidency, we will be challenged to give meaning to his slogan "Make America Great Again."

CHAPTER 1

Theodore Roosevelt

"Master Therapist of the Middle Classes"

Theodore Roosevelt came to maturity in the Gilded Age, a time of national industrialization, labor strife, and concentrated wealth. Diamond Jim Brady was an emblematic figure of the era—an unrefined mogul whom Roosevelt thought contemptible. Brady's diamond stickpin attached to a colorful cravat ostentatiously signaled his wealth. He made a fortune in the railroad business and the stock market, and became famous for his gluttony and corpulence. His meals at Delmonico's and Rector's, two of New York City's favorite restaurants of the rich and the famous at the start of the twentieth century, were undoubtedly exaggerated when described as multiple courses consisting of oysters, crabs, lobsters, steaks, vegetables, salads, and an array of desserts, all washed down by volumes of fresh orange juice and lemon soda. While Brady's self-indulgence offended some people, it appealed to others as a splendid example of the rags-to-riches story. The owner of Rector's described Brady as the best twenty-five customers he had. His stomach was reputed to be six times the size of a normal organ. He was supposed to have asked

Johns Hopkins University surgeons to consider replacing his stomach with an elephant's stomach. It was a legendary tale of vulgar self-indulgence that made Brady more of a hero than a crude glutton to millions of Americans who admired his opulence.[1] Brady was called the Prince of the Gilded Age.

Despite his contempt for Brady and other robber barons, TR was never the consummate foe of the capitalists for whom he expressed so much scorn. He thought labor was as much a menace to republican virtues as their business adversaries, and feared the rising power of organized workingmen. He saw them as "extremists," "radical fanatics," "the lunatic fringe," and "the professional criminal class." He aimed to tame both capital and labor by subjecting them to the mastery of the federal government, or what he called the "New Nationalism," perhaps better described as "paternalistic nationalism." His assertion of executive authority to rein in the country's competing economic forces set the stage for future presidents to uniformly claim ownership of prosperous surges. Of course, none of them have wanted to identify themselves with any downturns. And to defend themselves from bad publicity, presidents have worked to control the message. Roosevelt set the standard here as well by being the first president to cultivate the press. He would have been envious of later presidents' ability to directly reach millions of Americans by radio, television, and now electronic media.

For Roosevelt, all would be well as long as he could steer the ship of state. His grandiosity had few limits. It was said of him that he needed to be the baby at every christening, the groom at every wedding, and the corpse at every funeral. His need for ego satisfaction was insatiable. The British diplomat and TR friend Cecil Spring-Rice said, "You must always remember that the President is about six." Secretary of War Elihu Root tested the limits of TR's sense of humor when he told him, "You have made a very good start in life, and your friends have great hopes for you when you grow up." Roosevelt craved the hero's role as the soldier at the head of the charge, the moralist who led the country to a higher ground and the world to accept the rule of law as interpreted by him in the name of the United States. Rudyard Kipling, the English journalist and author, after listening to Roosevelt pontificate on every manner of thing in human affairs, said, "The universe seemed to be spinning around and Theodore was the spinner." The novelist Henry James called him "the very embodiment of noise." Roosevelt's behavior as chief executive gave license to his successors to think of themselves as masters of the universe[2] and believe that a president needed to be at the center of national and international attention.

Nothing was more exciting or rewarding for Roosevelt than soldiering. He loved any opportunity for battlefield heroics. He denounced pacifists as men weak in body and mind, and decried the many Americans who were schooled in isolationism and opposition to participation in any of the world's wars as lacking courage. He admired the saying, making it a hallmark of his presidency, "Speak softly and carry a big stick; you'll go far," though no one who heard him ever thought he did anything "softly."

In 1904, as the Republican convention met to nominate him, he seized the chance to give meaning to big-stick diplomacy. A bandit in Morocco named Raisuli kidnapped a Greek American, Ion Perdicaris, and demanded a ransom for his return. In response, Roosevelt sent a naval squadron to prod the Moroccan government into action. At the same time, he instructed the American consul to tell the sultan, "We want either Perdicaris alive or Raisuli dead." When Roosevelt's message was read to the delegates at the convention, they responded with cheers of approval for the president's decisiveness.

And when news reached the country that Roosevelt's demand had won the release of Perdicaris and other hostages, Americans across the country cheered as well.

Roosevelt himself was no stranger to combat. The war with Spain in 1898 had given him the chance to fulfill his fantasies of battlefield derring-do. Organizing the Rough Riders, a thousand skilled horsemen from the Southwest, into a cavalry brigade that fought in Cuba, he saw an opportunity to engage in what he called the "fighting edge" or "heroic virtues." He reflected on the joy of battle when he rode up a hill, waving his hat, and killing "a Spaniard with my own hand." "Look at those damn Spanish dead," he exalted. A comrade in the battle described him as "just reveling in victory and gore." Despite many accomplishments to come as president after Cuba, Roosevelt remembered his battlefield experience as "the great day of my life."[3] And he renewed his contempt for pacifists when the United States stood on the sidelines during the first three years of World War I. After the U.S. entered the fighting in 1917, when Roosevelt was fifty-nine years old, just two years before he died, he asked President Woodrow Wilson to let him lead a cavalry unit in France. To Roosevelt's dismay, Wilson refused his request, noting that battlefield conditions in the war largely outdated a cavalry charge.

It wasn't just the excitement of battle that captured his enthusiasm but the sense of being superior to the Spanish and everyone else he was in competition with. His reach for greatness seems to have grown out of some emotional desire to be viewed as top dog or the best at everything. In Roosevelt's time it resonated with the social Darwinist mind-set of the Victorian era. The British social biologist Herbert Spencer caught the spirit of the times when he coined the phrase "survival of the fittest," which described the progress of the human species from cavemen to modern gentlemen.

TR saw the doctrine as applying not only to individuals but also to nations and civilizations. He believed that the greatest achievements of an individual and a nation rested on contributions to human progress and, in his case, to what he did for humankind. It wasn't material wealth that marked out a man's life but whether he contributed to moral and social advancements. Some contemporaries lost patience with Roosevelt's grandiosity and pomposity. Speaker of the House Joe Cannon described him as "drunk on power," saying, "That fellow at the other end of the Avenue wants everything, from the birth of Christ to the death of the devil." The historian H. W. Brands describes TR's dominating personality during dinner-table conversations as allowing guests "little more than monosyllables in reply" to anything he said. It was all evidence of a self-centered character with an insatiable need for attention.

Roosevelt also saw a divide between superior and inferior races. Caucasian westerners were the best, while Africans and Asians were at the bottom of his rankings, though he considered the Japanese, who were imitating Europeans, much superior to the Chinese, who were under west European, Russian, and Japanese control. Roosevelt aimed to ensure that America stood in the front rank.

TR's presidency was distinguished by his groundbreaking, but not always aboveboard, executive actions. Supreme Court justice Oliver Wendell Holmes said of Roosevelt, "He was very likeable, a big figure, a rather ordinary intellect, with extraordinary gifts, a shrewd and I think *pretty unscrupulous politician* [my italics]." Holmes added, "What the boys liked about Roosevelt is that he doesn't give a damn for the law." Joe Cannon echoed Holmes when he said that Roosevelt's "got no more use for the Constitution than a tomcat has for a marriage license." It gave grounds for future presidents to do the same with as much sleight of hand as they could muster.

Roosevelt came to the presidency by chance. Accepting William McKinley's offer to be his running mate in 1900, TR's mostly ceremonial position as vice president made him the automatic successor to the Oval Office when an assassin's bullet killed McKinley in September 1901. But Roosevelt was prepared to assume command. He had won a statewide gubernatorial election in New York, then the country's most populous state, as well as appointment to national offices on the Civil Service Commission and as assistant secretary of the navy. When Republican boss Mark Hanna described him as a "damn cowboy" after McKinley's assassination, he ignored the fact that Roosevelt was a seasoned politician who understood the need for public backing if he was to succeed in the presidency. Indeed, TR proved to be brilliant at mobilizing popular support. Like "circus impresario P. T. Barnum," Roosevelt understood how to "put on a corking good show." He was a vessel of unbounded energy: A British visitor to the United States compared him to "Niagara Falls . . . both great wonders of nature." As historian William E. Leuchtenburg explained, TR was a study in "self-promotion . . . He made sure that he was front-page news. . . . As tales of his antics and adventures circulated, Roosevelt became the first president to be treated as a media personality. . . . His flashing teeth, pince-nez, bushy mustache, and frenetic gestures proved irresistible to caricaturists."

Roosevelt understood that political campaigns were never a model of decorum. Once elected, however, presidents, eager to maintain the dignity of the office, have resisted using derogatory language in public about opponents, though they would give private vent to their anger. Theodore Roosevelt, for example, could be scathing about Congress, privately writing a friend, "There are several eminent statesmen at the other end of Pennsylvania Avenue whom I would gladly lend to the Russian government, if they care to expend them as bodyguards for Grand Dukes whenever there was a likelihood of dynamite bombs being exploded." He was no less abrasive about some foreign leaders. But in public, he was a model of tact and decorum.

It was also a time when the press was much more under a president's command. Journalists were forbidden to quote a president directly unless given permission, and those who did so without approval were barred from further access to the White House. And Roosevelt was taken at his word when he denied the accuracy of a quote. Respect for the president's word was simply not in question. Every occupant of the White House understood that presidential credibility was an essential ingredient of majority rule.

Not only did Roosevelt see the office as an opportunity for self-promotion, he also saw it as a chance to right national wrongs. He took constructive actions that fulfilled his vision of a dynamic chief executive, creating long-term federal agencies that put the Washington government at the center of American politics. Where the states, counties, and cities were more influential than the federal authority in the post–Civil War era, TR changed this in order to reduce if not eliminate the country's economic and social ills. In short, he expanded the powers of the presidency—both positively and negatively—in ways that have lasted to this day.

In 1902, a coal miners' strike that underscored the fierce conflict between labor and management of the time threatened to deprive most Americans of winter heating supplies. Roosevelt stepped in to mediate the 163-day clash. He wrote the British historian George Trevelyan, "Somehow or other we shall have to work out methods of controlling the big corporations without paralyzing the energies of the business community and of preventing any tyranny on the part of the labor unions while cordially assisting in every proper effort made by the wage workers to better themselves by combinations." When he arranged a settlement by establishing an arbitration commission to mediate differences, under the rubric of the "Square Deal," it made the president a national hero, and the federal government the defender of the people and a fair arbiter of national disputes.

His leadership was notable for its evenhandedness, or at least an effort to convince the public of that. He explained that he was not intent on destroying the country's large trusts but on regulating them. The nation's corporations, he argued, were "an inevitable development of modern industrialism." His handling of his most famous antitrust action, the reining in of the Northern Securities holding company, a railroad monopoly in the Northwest, won Roosevelt additional popular support for his decisive use of presidential power. As important, his prosecution of the company did nothing to impede the national economy. "It was a brilliant stroke of publicity that could hardly have been resisted even by a more conservative politician," historian Richard Hofstadter wrote. It was all part of what Roosevelt called the square dealing that endeared him to the public. In a time of demoralization about politics, which was seen as corrupt and captive to special interests, Wisconsin Progressive Robert M. LaFollette, Sr. said TR "is the ablest living interpreter of . . . the superficial public sentiment of a given time," or as another commentator said, he understood the "psychology of the mutt." In Hofstadter's description, TR was "the master therapist of the middle classes."

His popularity with the public, and voters in particular, reflected itself in the 1904 presidential election, when he defeated Democrat judge Alton B. Parker by 2.5 million votes out of 12.7 million, then the largest popular vote percentage difference in U.S. history. Parker commanded only 38 percent of the general ballots and won the support of only the solid Democratic or ex-Confederate South. Roosevelt described himself as, of course, pleased but "astound[ed]" by "such a sweep." And yet Roosevelt couldn't accept that anyone or any part of the country would oppose him. He dismissed the vote across the South as the product of "fraud and violence" best described as a "farce." He salved his ego by telling his son that he had "the greatest popular majority and the greatest electoral majority ever given to a candidate for President."

Roosevelt gained and maintained the public's backing with reforms that regulated the railroads (the Elkins and Hepburn Acts); a Department of Commerce and Labor partly committed to exposing business corruption; regulation of the food and drug processing industries with a Meat Inspection Act; the creation of the Food and Drug Administration (FDA); regulations overseeing children's and women's working conditions; and conservation measures that included the Reclamation Service, the National Forest Service, the Antiquities Act restricting the use of public lands for private gain, and the creation of five national parks. He has been seen as the greatest conservationist president in the country's history, his only competitor being his successor and distant cousin Franklin D. Roosevelt.[4]

While Roosevelt championed progressive causes and spoke in ways that reflected public sentiment, he was no novice when it came to deceit and slander. When he faced a campaign of opposition to a Bureau of Corporations set up to expose business abuses of the public good, he launched an attack on John D. Rockefeller with an invented document revealing the robber baron's alleged malfeasance. Presidential deceptions bring to mind what Lincoln said about political lying: "You can fool all the people some of the time, and some of the people all the time, but you cannot fool all of the people all of the time."[5]

Roosevelt's most effective deceptions were in defending his foreign policies, where he felt free to disguise his actions with high-minded rhetoric, knowing that international affairs commanded limited public attention. He saw his foreign policies as serving the national interest, especially in asserting U.S. power in the Caribbean and in Central America, acquiring control of the Panama Canal territory, mediating the end of the Russo-Japanese War with the 1905 Treaty of Portsmouth, arbitrating a Franco-German conflict in 1905–6 over North Africa, and describing the Great White Fleet circumnavigating the globe between 1907 and 1909 as being on a peace mission.

Much of what he did rested on the assumption that he enjoyed the approval of average Americans across the country. In 1903, when he spent three months visiting every far western state, he recalled his earlier days in the Badlands. More important, he took satisfaction from speaking to "thoroughly good American citizens—a term I can use . . . without being thought demagogic," he wrote John Hay, his secretary of state. The people who had come to hear him speak were "rough-coated, hard-headed, gaunt, sinewy farmers and hired hands from all their neighborhood. . . . For all the superficial differences between us, down at bottom these men and I think a good deal alike, or at least have the same ideals, and I am always sure of reaching them in speeches. . . . They all felt I was their man, their old friend." It was a testimony to Roosevelt's confidence in his ability to win the support of most Americans. But it also illustrated his affinity for superlatives about himself and everything he touched.[6]

A major consideration for Roosevelt in keeping a hold on popular opinion was to ensure that national security actions would not cost the country blood and treasure. Nothing seemed more important to TR than maintaining U.S. dominance in the Americas and building and controlling an isthmian canal that would make the United States a two-ocean power. At a time when advanced industrial nations were vying for spheres of control around the world that served their economic and security interests, Roosevelt believed it essential for the United States to join the scramble for world standing and power.

In 1902, German economic penetration of Latin America had made Roosevelt apprehensive about Berlin's intentions and heightened his determination to fend off its reach for influence in the hemisphere. In December, when Germany and Britain blockaded Venezuelan ports to compel payments on bonds, Roosevelt bristled at the thought of violations of the Monroe Doctrine, which had made the hemisphere a U.S. sphere of influence. Knowing that American public opinion was decidedly antagonistic to the Germans, Roosevelt pressured Berlin with a vague threat of war into arbitrating the crisis. When it succeeded, he put aside any discussion of national interest to explain the outcome in terms of "service to the cause of arbitration" and to a "code of international ethics." It proved to be a pattern for how he cultivated public opinion in building support for aggressive action overseas.[7]

German retreat encouraged Roosevelt to be more aggressive about building a canal, which he considered among the most important things he could do as president. Because so many Americans were unenthusiastic about foreign involvement that might require gunboat diplomacy, which Colombia's rejection of a treaty giving the U.S. rights to build a canal across the Panamanian Isthmus (Panama then being a province of Colombia) made more likely, Roosevelt emphasized that a canal was one "for the ages," something "of consequence, not merely decades, but centuries hence." He responded to the Colombia action by saying, "I do not think that the Bogotá lot of jack rabbits should be allowed permanently to bar one of the future highways of civilization." He told John Hay that, "In some shape or way," they needed "to secure the Panama route without further dealings with the foolish and homicidal corruptionists in Bogotá." In short, according to Roosevelt, whatever the U.S. did during his presidency would be the product not of America's selfish interests but of high-minded ideals benefiting peoples everywhere. Building a canal, he said, was "justified in morals and . . . in law." He said nothing publicly about strategic and economic advantages for the U.S. in building and controlling a canal, the most compelling reasons for Roosevelt's Panama actions.

A Panamanian revolution would open the way to U.S. acquisition of a canal zone and construction of an isthmian route between the Atlantic and Pacific Oceans. Although Roosevelt took pains to deny any role in facilitating and defending a Panamanian rebellion to separate itself from Colombia, his use of a U.S. cruiser to block Colombian forces from suppressing the uprising made the difference in assuring its success. And Roosevelt would claim, "By every law, human and divine, Panama was right in her position." He was not content just to get the canal; Roosevelt also wanted everyone to agree that it was the right thing to do. He described opponents of his action as "a small body of shrill eunuchs" and declared the canal "immensely to the interest of the world, and in accord with the fundamental laws of righteousness."

When Roosevelt made the case to his cabinet, Attorney General Philander Knox told him, "I would not let so great an achievement suffer from any taint of legality." Secretary of War Elihu Root joined in twitting the president with a memorable barb. "Have I defended myself?" TR had asked. "You certainly have," Root declared. "You have shown that you were accused of seduction and you have conclusively proved that you were guilty of rape."[8]

Roosevelt defended himself by asserting that "our course was . . . in absolute accord with the highest standard of international morality." It appealed to America's dominant isolationist and idealistic sentiments. Yet if he and the public were going to see him as a great president, he needed to assert his affinity for realpolitik. Eight years after he seized the canal zone, he acknowledged his high-handedness in acquiring control of the Panama territory when he declared in a postpresidential speech at the University of California at Berkeley, "I took the canal." He also described it as the greatest engineering feat in history—a self-tribute to his imperiousness and greatness as a world leader.

His remarks resonated with his Roosevelt Corollary to the Monroe Doctrine, announced in his 1904 State of the Union message. Animated by what he saw as Germany's interference in Venezuela's failure to meet its debt payments, TR declared the area a zone of U.S. interest in which we would keep order or act as a regional policeman. In brief, where Monroe had declared the Americas out-of-bounds to European colonization, Roosevelt interpreted Monroe's doctrine to mean that the U.S. was the sole power assigned to enforce the region's law and order. Indeed, he described it as America's duty "to police these [Latin] countries in the interest of order and civilization."[9]

Roosevelt's statement was an expression of America's imperial ambitions similar to what other world powers—Belgium, Great Britain, France, Germany, Holland, Italy, Portugal, Spain, Russia, and Japan—believed essential to their future safety and prosperity. But because a majority of Americans remained convinced that isolationism was the safest and morally best course for the United States, all foreign policy actions had to be cast in the spirit of advancing civilized standards rather than any self-serving ones. Bordered by vast oceans on the east and the west and weaker neighbors to the north and south in Canada and Mexico, Americans enjoyed "free security" and imagined foreign affairs in terms of a civilized standard or rule of law rather than power politics. Roosevelt's international ambitions had to be reframed accordingly.

In 1904, when Japan's negotiations with Russia over spheres of control in Korea and Manchuria reached a deadlock, the Japanese fleet bombarded and decimated Russia's fleet at Port Arthur in Manchuria. Because Russia's czarist government and imperial aggression was unpopular in the United States, Roosevelt reflected American opinion when he said, "I was thoroughly well pleased with the Japanese victory." But what he believed and never said publicly was that the Japanese were serving our interests. At the same time, he saw a Japanese victory over Russia and control of the resource-rich Manchuria as a threat to American commerce, or what he called the "yellow peril" as opposed to the "Slav peril." He feared "that Japan might become intoxicated with victory and embark on a career of insolence and aggression."[10] He favored an open door in China—that is, no zones of control across Asia's largest country, which assured American opportunity for trade in all parts of China, but especially Manchuria.

The conflict lasted more than a year, and though Japan won every battle on land and at sea, both sides were exhausted and receptive to peace talks. Japan was facing bankruptcy over the costs of the war and hoped to extract indemnity payments from Saint Petersburg, while revolutionary upheaval over its military defeats was dogging Russia's czarist rule.

Determined to protect U.S. interests in the Pacific and East Asia, specifically the Philippines, where Roosevelt feared Japanese interference to expel us, and commerce in Manchuria, where he saw Japan and Russia intent on spheres of full economic control, Roosevelt had no intention of entering the conflict except as a peacemaker. Any military involvement in a distant imperial conflict would be highly unpopular in the United States. By contrast, a peace initiative would resonate with a majority of Americans as fulfilling the country's highest ideals as a force not for self-aggrandizement but for the international good.

Roosevelt invited Saint Petersburg and Tokyo to send delegates to the United States for a negotiated settlement in the port city of Portsmouth, New Hampshire. The belligerents wondered, Why not a site on the West Coast of the United States in a city fronting the Pacific Ocean; or Washington, D.C., the U.S. capital? But Portsmouth was across from Kittery, Maine, where a shipyard served as the principal base of the U.S. fleet. The talks therefore occurred with the fleet on display to the belligerents' delegates. It was a calculated gesture on TR's part to show off American naval power and demonstrate that the U.S. was prepared to defend its interests in Asia.

Roosevelt did not come to the talks in Portsmouth but kept in close touch with the differences roiling the two sides. In response, he solicited the German kaiser's help in pressuring Russia and communicated directly with the two governments' leaders to reach a settlement. Although both sides were persuaded more by the unsettling prospect of continuing the war than by Roosevelt's hectoring, the settlement made clear that the United States was a power to be reckoned with in the Pacific, and Roosevelt emerged as the principal victor in the talks. He even received the Nobel Peace Prize in 1906 for his efforts, the first American president to be so honored.[11]

The Portsmouth Treaty and Nobel Peace Prize spurred Roosevelt's determination to make the United States and himself an enduring major influence on the world stage. In 1905, while Roosevelt maneuvered to arrange an end to the Russo-Japanese War, a conflict between Germany and France over Morocco in North Africa threatened to lead to a European war. Angry at French moves to bring Morocco under its economic control, Germany's Kaiser Wilhelm publicly took issue with Paris's indifference to Berlin's interests. Mindful of Roosevelt's requests to him to pressure Russia into a settlement with Tokyo, the kaiser sent word to TR that he was tired of France's "bullying" and believed it needed to be confronted before it provoked a military conflict. He asked the president to pressure France into a conference of the European powers that would agree on an open door to Morocco's commerce. He told Roosevelt through his ambassador in Washington, "He would have to choose between the possibility of a war with France and the examining of those conditions which France may have to propose, so as to avoid a war."

While Roosevelt saw "no real [U.S.] interest in Morocco," he worried about the outbreak of a conflict between Europe's two strongest continental powers. With the Russo-Japanese conflict still unsettled, he thought a European outbreak would be "a real calamity" in "a world conflagration" that could do incalculable harm to France, which he thought would be mauled by a German invasion as had occurred in the Franco-Prussian war a generation earlier. Roosevelt urged France to agree to a conference, and when it did, he pressed the kaiser to accept, telling him that he had "won a great triumph . . . and I earnestly hope that he can see his way clear to accept it as the triumph it is." But Roosevelt had to make an additional démarche before the two sides would agree to meet at the Spanish port city of Algeciras in January 1906. Seen as an honest broker, Roosevelt successfully proposed that both sides enter the talks with no agendas. While it offered no guarantee that the adversaries would find common ground, it at least brought them to the table.

The negotiations lasted three months and came close to breaking down. Although Roosevelt kept his role in the negotiations secret, he was a crucial force in arranging the settlement. He laid out four points for the negotiators to discuss. After two months of back-and-forth, France and Germany agreed on three of them, but the kaiser resisted signing on to the fourth. Roosevelt then threatened to make the correspondence between him and Berlin public, which he predicted would greatly embarrass the German side. He also promised to give the kaiser ample credit for a settlement. Although the back-channel nature of Roosevelt's messages to Berlin and Paris made his influence on the talks in Algeciras less notable than his very public role in the Portsmouth Treaty, it retrospectively demonstrated his skill in international affairs. TR knew when to publicize his actions and when to work behind the scenes.

Nowhere was Roosevelt's skill in combining American self-interest under the cloak of idealism more evident than in his decision to send the Great White Fleet—America's battleships—on a global tour. The backdrop to the fleet's journey, which lasted for fourteen months from December 1907 to February 1909, was tensions between the United States and Japan triggered by anti-Japanese sentiment in California, including the segregation of Japanese children from white students in public schools. The Chinese Exclusion Act of 1882, which had barred Chinese immigration to the U.S., and Japan's military victories over Russia provoked Japanese demonstrations against any signs of discrimination in the United States against Asians, but especially Japanese migrants. The Roosevelt administration negotiated a gentlemen's agreement with Tokyo that discouraged any discriminatory measures against Japanese in the U.S., in return for which Japan agreed to withhold passports from any of their citizens proposing to migrate to America.

None of this, however, was sufficient to quiet the nationalist rumblings in the United States and Japan. Roosevelt quietly threatened retaliation against U.S. newspapers stirring up trouble. He told his friend Massachusetts senator Henry Cabot Lodge that "I shall continue to do everything I can by politeness and consideration to the Japs to offset the worse than criminal stupidity of the San Francisco mob, the San Francisco press, and such papers as the New York *Herald*." Similarly, because he thought the Japanese had "about the same proportion of prize jingo fools that we have," he hoped to quiet war talk in Japan with a show of American naval power. And though the presence of the battle fleet in the Pacific was advertised as nothing more than maneuvers, it registered in Tokyo as an undisguised threat. To mute any suggestion that Roosevelt was spoiling for a war with Japan, he disarmed pacifist antagonism with an announcement that the sixteen battleships and assorted other ships would circumnavigate the globe and make goodwill visits to numerous foreign ports, including some in Japan. Roosevelt later asserted that his "prime purpose was to impress the American people" that America was not a warlike country but an advanced industrial nation capable of a feat that no other country had dared try. To make his point with the public, he took pains to enlist sympathetic newspapermen to travel with the fleet and send back positive stories along the way. The fleet admiral screened all articles before their release. The fleet's journey was a constant source of positive news for the administration as well as a signal to the world that the United States was a world power.[12]

* * *

No president is so wedded to an earlier chief that he tries to imitate the same actions or follow the exact same policies. Yet knowing about the effective behavior of earlier presidents is certainly of interest to most presidents, though they are mindful of creating a fresh narrative about their own performance. Theodore Roosevelt's credibility with the American people and foreign officials has become an essential standard. Regardless of what Roosevelt said in private, which his closest advisers kept under wraps, and despite the fact that he deceived the public about his full intentions, he shrewdly framed his policies so as to assure the trust of other heads of government and the American public. It was a demonstration of how much Roosevelt believed that he could not govern effectively without majority approval in the United States and a reputation for reliability by other leaders—whether allies or adversaries. It is a lesson all presidents do well to recall. In fact, the Roosevelt presidency went far to shape the presidency from his day to ours—both in its constructive actions and its misuse of power.

The most compelling development in shaping future presidential behavior was not strictly what he achieved in domestic and foreign affairs, though this counted a great deal, but his appeal as a public personality who excited national interest in himself and Washington events. Roosevelt could have been a regular voice on radio, or a reality TV star, or a larger-than-life presence on social media. But even with just the newspapers of his time, he became an almost daily source of attention and interest. Not every future president could possibly match Roosevelt's status as a hero, and he made an indelible mark on the office. He set the standard for every future president to command center stage on a daily basis. Yet Roosevelt's need for attention was a problem for future presidents, especially with the rise of the electronic media. The public's eagerness for a political drama created a challenge for presidents to constantly excite public interest or find something that encouraged public belief in the president's mastery of all problems. While it could serve a president's political standing, it also reduced his freedom to practice the political art of double-talk and behavior that crossed the line of appropriate action.

our better unselfish natures." More important, his speeches inspired Americans eager for idealistic leadership. "A cramped capacity for personal communication tortured and stunted his emotional life," Richard Hofstadter wrote. Yet "with masses of men Wilson was beautifully articulate, and in public he often got the sense of communion, if not affection, that he so missed in private."[1]

Wilson, like so many other presidents, craved power not only because it gave him a sense of superiority but also because it gave him the chance to improve America and the world. In their campaigns, other presidents used high-minded rhetoric to bond with their audiences, but it was unclear exactly how they intended to move the country forward. By contrast, Wilson had a clear vision of how he hoped to advance the nation's standing at home and abroad.

He believed that a more humane society was vital in enhancing the nation's greatness and international appeal. It continued what Roosevelt had initiated and set a high standard for future presidents. Still, Wilson began his presidency with few convictions about American contributions to international affairs beyond promoting a more principled world, saying, "It would be an irony of fate if my administration had to deal chiefly with foreign problems, for all my preparation has been in domestic matters." He made his limited schooling in foreign relations apparent when he selected William Jennings Bryan as secretary of state. Bryan's parochialism and ignorance of European geography in particular registered on Lewis Einstein, the U.S. envoy in Constantinople in 1908. When he wished Bryan, who was on a tour of the Continent, a good trip through the Balkans, the seeding ground for World War I, Bryan asked, "The Balkans, what are they?" Einstein saw Bryan's response as astonishing provincialism. Ultimately, Wilson would settle on an agenda for reforming the world community, animating his actions in international affairs as they had in domestic matters by saying "that questions of government are moral questions." While Wilson proved to be an exceptionally able politician who could use rhetoric as a not always reliable political tool, he held the conviction that "we must believe the things we tell the children."

Wilson began his political career by saying that his "ambition" was "to become an invigorating and enlightening power in the world of political thought." Although he launched his reach for public office, as most politicians did, through law studies, he quickly abandoned a vocation he viewed as pedestrian and uninspiring. Instead, he chose an academic career as a political scientist by earning a Johns Hopkins Ph.D. in 1886 at the age of thirty.[2]

His career as a professor and university administrator formed a stark contrast with almost all his presidential predecessors and successors, except for Dwight Eisenhower, who served as president of Columbia University, and Barack Obama, who taught at the University of Chicago Law School. Despite considerable success as an academic, Wilson never found this part of his profession very satisfying. While earning his Ph.D. and publishing his first book, *Congressional Government*, he taught for three years at Bryn Mawr in Pennsylvania, a women's college, saying "lecturing to young women of the present generation [who cannot vote] on the history and principles of politics is about as appropriate and profitable as would be lecturing to stonemasons on the evolution of fashion in dress." In 1888, he accepted a professorship at Wesleyan University in Connecticut before winning appointment in 1890 as a professor at Princeton University, his undergraduate college.

After twelve years, having established himself as the most popular lecturer and a leading light on campus, he became president of Princeton and embarked on a series of progressive reforms, including the unsuccessful abolition of the undemocratic eating clubs. His service at Princeton opened the way in 1910 to his candidacy and two-year term as governor of New Jersey. He won the Democratic nomination for governor with a "stirring peroration" that described America as "not distinguished so much by its wealth and material power as by the fact that it was born with an ideal, a purpose to serve mankind." As the Kansas editor William Allen White said, the Progressives aimed "to end the reign of the plutocrats and pass laws that would make the federal government 'an agency of human welfare.' Lord," he added, "how we did like that phrase."[3]

Wilson's high-minded rhetoric throughout his gubernatorial campaign helped him defeat his Republican opponent by a fifty-thousand-vote margin out of more than four hundred thousand. No captive of his party's unpopular bosses, Wilson turned against them in his administration of the governorship. The New Jersey Democratic boss Jim Smith described Wilson as adroit in "the art of foul play." James Nugent, the party's state chairman and ally of Smith, accused Wilson of being "an ingrate and a liar." The clash with machine politicians served Wilson's ambitions to run for president, as did his record as governor. He described his election as a repudiation of boss politics funded by an alliance between big business and political machines; it was "a victory of the 'progressives' of both parties." As governor, Wilson favored popular progressive reforms—public utility regulation and greater power to the people through democratization of politics with direct primaries and other electoral reforms; campaign finance reforms; as well as women's and child labor laws to protect the vulnerable from exploitation.[4]

When talk of him running for president began to mount, he declared, as serious candidates usually did, "I do not *want* to be president. There is too little play in it, too little time for one's friends, too

much distasteful publicity and fuss and frills." Wilson's pronouncement was little more than rhetoric by a man eager to become president. Since part of the political process was to disguise your intent to
run to discourage an early campaign against your candidacy, no one
attacked a future candidate's credibility for having denied his interest. In fact, it was considered smart politics. But there was also some
truth to it. Privately, Wilson said that while "he did not dread the
burden of high office, what depressed" him about being president
was "the thought of all the trivia and distractions he would have to
endure—hateful work that counted for nothing."[5]

Wilson understood that the path to the Democratic nomination in
1912 would require shifting to more liberal pronouncements that won
the support of populist William Jennings Bryan and those who had
backed his three earlier Democratic Party nominations. But the contest for the prize was a hard-fought battle that pitted Wilson against
the Speaker of the House, Missouri's Champ Clark, and the House
majority leader, Alabama's Oscar Underwood. While Wilson's turn
toward progressivism served his purposes, a split in the then-liberal
Republican Party between incumbent president William Howard
Taft and the former chief executive Theodore Roosevelt (who ran as
a candidate in the newly formed Bull Moose Party) improved Wilson's chances of success, but also raised questions about his ability
to best Roosevelt. Although Wilson barely won the nomination, the
competition demonstrated his keen political skills. Having opposed
Bryan's runs for the presidency, including in a 1907 letter that declared, "Would that we could . . . knock Mr. Bryan once and for all
into a cocked hat!" Wilson openly courted and praised Bryan up to
and during the party's convention in the summer of 1912, including a
rumored secret promise to make Bryan secretary of state despite his
parochialism. What also served Wilson's reach for the nomination

was the absence of a track record in national affairs—a not uncommon advantage in presidential contests.

Nevertheless, Wilson's campaign against Taft and Roosevelt was no cakewalk. Wilson knew that he was in for a tough fight when the highly popular Roosevelt played to national emotions with a speech at his newly formed Bull Moose Party's convention in Chicago in which he invoked the familiar religious rallying cry: "We stand at Armageddon and we battle for the Lord." With the unpopular Taft an also-ran, the real contest was between Wilson and Roosevelt to see who would make the most compelling case for a progressive agenda. Wilson understood that he could not outdo TR in certain respects, saying that he did not measure up alongside TR's "vivid" persona, with his "human traits and red corpuscles." Wilson saw himself as "a vague, conjectural personality," notable for his "academic prepossessions." A journalist who met him for the first time said that "the hand he gave me to shake felt like a ten-cent pickled mackerel in brown paper." Yet Wilson took encouragement from the thought that he could provide a more coherent set of progressive proposals that would eclipse Roosevelt's blustery rhetoric. Besides, it was a time when a rationally based agenda resonated with millions of educated voters.

A crisis occurred for Wilson in mid-October when a deranged individual shot Roosevelt as he was giving a speech in Milwaukee. Roosevelt's bravery in continuing to speak until the loss of blood forced him to stop reinforced his reputation as a courageous man with a proven track record of leadership. But Wilson blunted some of this by suspending his campaign in deference to Roosevelt. It resonated with voters as honorable and generous. Whether it affected the outcome of the election is impossible to say. (There were no opinion polls until 1935, and even then they were less than reliable.)

The election turned on a weakened Republican Party split between Roosevelt and Taft. Wilson won with only 42 percent of the popular vote. Although Wilson and Roosevelt drew a line between themselves with what Wilson called the New Freedom and Roosevelt called the New Nationalism, most observers saw little significant ideological difference separating them. The famous Kansas editor William Allen White later said it was like "that fantastic imaginary gulf that has existed between tweedle-dum and tweedle-dee," especially after Wilson adopted so much of Roosevelt's policy during his administration. The campaign, however, did reveal differences in emphasis between the two front-runners, with Roosevelt depicting an economy that needed greater federal government regulation and Wilson describing a national need for more radical reforms promoting greater competition and less regulation. Ultimately, voters opted for the newer, less well-known Wilson ahead of the better-known Roosevelt, who had become too familiar a face to convince a restive public that he would be as innovative in an unprecedented third term as the less-recognizable Wilson.

Wilson's first term from 1913 to 1916 was a notable success. He had a 300 to 134 majority in the House and an eight-seat advantage in the Senate that he used to pass several significant laws. Instead of sustaining the divide in the country provoked by the campaign, Wilson promoted greater unity by appealing to TR progressives with a call "for action in four areas: conservation of natural resources, equal access to raw materials, equal access to credit, and reform of the tariff."

In the first days of his presidency, Wilson broke with tradition by appearing at a joint congressional session to urge passage of a tariff law. The custom of presidents sending written messages to Congress, which dated from Thomas Jefferson's presidency, fell before Wilson's determination to show the legislators that the chief executive had a human face. He said, "I am very glad indeed to have this opportunity to address the two Houses directly and to verify for myself the impression that the President of the United States is a person, not a mere department of the Government hailing Congress from some isolated island of jealous power, sending messages, not speaking naturally and with his own voice—that he is a human being trying to cooperate with other human beings in a common service." Although Wilson's appearance aroused some complaints about a pronouncement from the throne and an assault on the separation of powers, Wilson used the event to press the case successfully for lower tariff rates promoting freer trade.

His appearance set a precedent for future presidents. Even in the age of radio and television, when presidents have become much more familiar figures than in Wilson's time, a personal appearance makes a strong impression on an audience. When Franklin Roosevelt served as governor of New York, he made a point, despite being paralyzed from the waist down, of visiting out-of-the-way communities. It was meant to convince people of his competence but also to endear him to ordinary citizens, as were his radio broadcasts or "fireside chats." And when Lyndon Johnson visited a tornado-damaged Indiana, for example, a local paper praised him for showing "personal concern" as someone "to be seen and spoken to." It was evidence that he cared. By contrast, when George H. W. Bush seemed mystified by the checkout counter at a supermarket, it suggested a president with little understanding of people's everyday lives. Or when George W. Bush was photographed on Air Force One looking down on flood-ravaged New Orleans, it conveyed a message of detachment or of a president lacking concern for flood victims.

Although lacking modern electronic technology to communicate with the public, Wilson was not without techniques for capturing public approval, but it rested on more than sloganeering. Passage of the Underwood Tariff, which ended twenty years of special-interest barriers to international commerce, was the first of Wilson's victories. Tariff reform that reduced federal revenue opened the way to the income tax amendment to the Constitution that compelled wealthy Americans to support public services. Wilson said, "What this country needs above everything else is a body of laws which will look after the men who are on the make rather than the men who are already made." It was Wilson's way of saying that we need to rein in the excesses of corporations and political bosses and promote greater economic opportunity, which he did with passage of the Clayton antitrust law and the Federal Farm Loan Act, and creation of the Federal Reserve Bank and the Federal Trade Commission. He also humanized the American industrial system with support for labor in the La Follette Seaman's Act, the Adamson Act limiting exploitation of railroad workers with an eight-hour day, a child labor law reducing the abuse of children working in unsafe conditions and at slave wages, and gave women a greater political and social voice with the Nineteenth Amendment's guarantee of voting rights. "The first Wilson administration, in fact," Richard Hofstadter wrote, "produced more positive legislative achievements than any administration since the days of Alexander Hamilton" with "an almost absolute authority over Congress." Moreover, it set a standard for what would come in the FDR and LBJ administrations.[6]

On race relations, however, Wilson, demonstrating his southern roots, was never progressive. His administration was notable for having introduced segregation in Washington, D.C. Most of these initiatives came from Wilson's southern cabinet officers, but though advocates of racial equality protested against the setting up of separate facilities for blacks and whites throughout the government and the reduction in black civil servants, Wilson turned a blind eye to the practice. It won approval from influential southerners in Congress, who voted for Wilson's legislative program in exchange for his support of segregation.

To modernize or bring the presidency into the twentieth century, Wilson also pioneered twice-a-week press conferences, meeting with reporters sixty-four times in 1913 and again in 1914. Although he had his share of tensions with the White House press corps, he also found the meetings an enjoyable exercise in combat or matching wits with journalists hungry for printable news. He never complained about "fake news," but he did object to leaks from these off-the-record sessions.

Though it was no guarantee of success in the highest office, Wilson came to the presidency with significant administrative experience. He also relied on Colonel Edward House of Texas to help guide him in managing both domestic and foreign affairs. Wilson described House as "my second personality. He is my independent self. His thoughts and mine are one." Wilson's conviction that House was not a "first-class" mind and was a "counselor" but not a "statesman" convinced Wilson that he was in charge and remained the dominant figure in the administration throughout his two terms.

On foreign affairs, Wilson shared the limitation of inexperience with several future presidents. It became an open secret in the early days of his term, though Wilson masked his "America First" nationalism with talk of idealism that had also hidden Roosevelt's affinity for putting the national interest above all else. As a believer in peaceful dealings with nations around the globe and America as a beacon opposing international power politics, Wilson, unlike Roosevelt, struggled to make sense of the harsh realities animating self-serving nationalism.

Wilson distinguished himself by never appeasing dictators. With the best of intentions, Wilson pledged in a Mobile, Alabama, address in October 1913, seven months into his term, to free "the southern republics from the strangle hold of foreign concessionaires." Yet he was at sea in his dealings with Latin America and especially Mexico. As Wilson's biographer Arthur S. Link wrote, "the administration . . . found itself so entangled by previous commitments and especially by its own inconsistencies that it violated all its generous professions in its relations with Mexico, Central America, and the island countries. The years from 1913 to 1921 witnessed intervention by the State Department and the navy on a scale that had never before been contemplated, even by such alleged imperialists as Theodore Roosevelt and William Howard Taft."[7]

Wilson's troubles with Mexico were the result of his inexperience and moralistic preachments that proved to be poor substitutes for realistic foreign policies. When Wilson said "I am going to teach the South American republics to elect good men," it was more the pronouncement of an imperialist than of a good neighbor encouraging political reforms across Latin America. But the outbreak and course of the First World War beginning in August 1914 pushed Mexican problems aside.

No foreign problem generated greater difficulties for Wilson and Bryan than the European war. Wilson at once offered to mediate the conflict, but patriotic enthusiasm among the combatants for war outran any interest in peace. Wilson and Bryan, horrified by the German invasion and destruction of Belgian towns and artifacts, thought "the world . . . seems gone mad." It was in a state of "general wreck and distemper," with "barbarism" erasing "centuries of civilization." Wilson urged Americans, many of whom had family backgrounds in one of the belligerent countries, "to be impartial in thought as well as in action." Wilson's neutrality extended to selling weapons to all belligerents. It enriched some Americans and undercut assertions of refusal to take sides by providing far more arms to Britain and France than to Germany or Austria-Hungary. In addition, Wilson told British ambassador Cecil Spring-Rice that if Germany won the war, "the United States would be forced to enlarge its defenses to a point that would be fatal to American democracy." It was hardly a statement calculated to demonstrate American neutrality. Similarly, although impartiality for loans to belligerents was official U.S. policy, U.S. banks advanced lines of credit to the British and French at a hundred times the amounts provided to Germany to buy arms.

As depicted in Jean Renoir's brilliant 1937 film, *The Grand Illusion*, the view from Europe across national lines was initially of a civilized conflict between gentlemen—a view held by Europe's aristocrats who saw combat as an honorable matter. In the film, two French aviators who have been shot down and captured are invited to lunch with German officers, where they sing their respective national anthems, "La Marseillaise" followed by "Deutschland über Alles," suggesting that this would be a war between officers and gentlemen. At the same time, the futility and pointlessness of the conflict had little appeal to most citizens thrilled by the pageantry of sending men off to fight. Only when the war turned into the brutal trench combat that cost millions of lives and untold suffering did people come to Wilson's view of a descent into barbarism. Though it would take a while for this reality to set in, the war quickly refuted Englishman Norman Angell's popular 1909 book, *The Great Illusion*, arguing that Europe would not see another war because their economies were so entwined that it would compel them to settle disputes peacefully.

Wilson's faux neutrality, which triggered Bryan's resignation in 1915 and Robert Lansing's appointment as secretary of state, combined with Germany's 1917 submarine campaign, would eventually bring the United States into the fighting. Wilson considered his decision to ask Congress for a war declaration in April 1917 as a defeat for all he had striven to achieve through politics. As he told a journalist friend on the eve of his request to Congress, the war would bring intolerance to America and would strain democratic traditions beyond durability. He feared that "the Constitution would not survive it; free speech and the right of assembly would go." He expected "the spirit of ruthless brutality . . . [to] enter into the very fiber of our national life, infecting Congress, the courts, the policeman on the beat, the man in the street."

To justify the price America would pay in the war—fifty-three thousand battlefield deaths—and the millions of other belligerents who were lost in the fighting, Wilson proposed to revolutionize the world international order. In January 1918, he outlined a fourteen-point peace plan that would make World War I the war to end all wars and the world safe for democracy. It was meant to produce a peace without victors, or "a peace between equals." French premier Georges Clemenceau joked that even the Lord had only ten commandments. The peace program was more an expression of Wilson's grandiosity than a realistic plan to head off future wars and extend democracy around the globe, though Wilson's vision of a world without war rested on substantive proposals with considerable appeal.

At the 1919 Versailles peace conference, however, Wilson's plans met a wall of resistance from his wartime allies intent on recouping some of their losses in the war and punishing the defeated governments with requirements for reparation payments and loss of territory—a contradiction of Wilson's insistence on a peace without victors and self-determination for all nations. At the end of the day, the principal element of Wilson's program left standing was a world league supposedly capable of collective security for all peoples. And even this could not withstand the loss of his party's Senate control in 1918. Having lost so much of his fourteen-point peace program at Versailles, he refused to concede any revisions for U.S. participation in the League of Nations. Consequently, entrance into the League fell short of the required two-thirds Senate vote and brought an end to Wilson's grand vision of a world transformed—at least by him.[8]

His failure was not just the result of political crosscurrents beyond his control but also his physical collapse. His health had been a longstanding problem beginning with a small stroke in 1896 when he was forty years old. During his Princeton presidency he had suffered minor strokes that temporarily immobilized a hand and impeded the vision in one eye. During Wilson's presidency, White House physician Admiral Cary Grayson tried to arrange Wilson's schedule so as to reduce tensions that might bring on a crippling stroke. Grayson hid his concerns from the president and hoped that the management of Wilson's daily activities could ward off any physical disaster.

In hiding Wilson's condition, Grayson was following a pattern established by President Grover Cleveland during his second term in 1893–97. At the start of Cleveland's term, his physicians discovered a cancer of the jaw and arranged for him to have it removed by surgeons operating on a private yacht on New York's East River. Skillfully replacing a part of the jaw with an undetectable prosthesis, the surgeons were able to hide Cleveland's ailment from the public. Only in 1917, after Cleveland had died and his surgeon published an article in the *Saturday Evening Post*, did the public learn the truth.

Wilson's medical history was more complicated and debilitating. The demands of the presidency and especially the war and peacemaking took a toll on Wilson's health. He was under constant strain and agitation over the failure of his Fourteen Points at the Versailles peace conference in 1919, and his domestic campaign for U.S. participation in the League of Nations put him on the edge of collapse. As he told the Belgian parliament, "The League of Nations is the child of this great war for right . . . and any nation which declines to adhere to this Covenant deliberately turns away from the most telling appeal that has ever been made to its conscience and its manhood."

In September 1919, as he spoke in Colorado on a national political tour urging Senate ratification of the peace treaty and the League, he suffered another small stroke. After canceling his tour and returning to Washington, a more debilitating stroke and a urinary blockage that further sapped his strength ended his ability to fight for Senate approval of joining the League.

His last eighteen months as president were a period of immobility and lost leadership. His physicians, wife, and associates hid the extent of his illness. A neurologist who examined him told reporters that the president "is very cheerful and takes an interest in what is going on." As Wilson biographer John Milton Cooper wrote, those "attending Wilson would issue only upbeat statements to the press, never mention or hint at a stroke, and refer only and vaguely to nervous exhaustion." The deception was a prelude to later acts of presidential dishonesty about health problems.

It was a great cover-up and would leave the country without genuine presidential leadership in a challenging time. Or as Cooper asserts, "The stroke and illness Woodrow Wilson suffered in October 1919 brought on the worst crisis of presidential disability in American history." Although the Constitution said that "in case of the Removal of the President from office, or his Death, Resignation, or Inability to discharge the Powers and Duties of the said Office, the same shall devolve on the Vice President," Wilson's cabinet decided against suspending the president's authority and transferring presidential powers to Vice President Thomas Marshall. Part of their reluctance to act rested on Marshall's lack of standing as a competent leader and his own doubts about his capacity to assume the burdens of the presidency.

Another Wilson biographer, Patricia O'Toole, summed up the situation: "With no clear path to follow, no substantive information on the president's condition, and a vice president dreading the prospect of assuming the presidency, Washington was reduced to watchful waiting." Although it was reasonably clear that Wilson would never get back to his earlier ability to govern the country, and Admiral Grayson suggested that Wilson resign at the start of 1920, Edith Wilson refused to agree. Led by the first lady, the White House maintained a facade of a president on the mend. Ike Hoover, the White House usher, who had a firsthand view of what was happening, anticipated a neurosurgeon's later conclusion that the president would never fully recover from his illness. In fact, two months after his stroke, Wilson remained so ill that he could not walk or sit up in a chair, and suffered dizzy spells, memory lapses, and double vision.[9]

And even if Wilson had recovered from his illness, it is doubtful that he would have found the wherewithal to lead the country into the League. In late 1919, the British economist John Maynard Keynes published *The Economic Consequences of the Peace*, predicting that the reparations demanded of Germany in the Versailles Treaty would bring on economic dislocations in Europe and eventually trigger another war. Keynes described Wilson as "a terrible negotiator . . . a blind and deaf Don Quixote." The book received wide attention in the United States, further diminishing Wilson's standing. Even a recovery would not have restored Wilson's skills as a politician capable of productive give and take.

Wilson's unrealism in 1920 extended to thoughts of running for a third term. He had fantasies of a deadlocked Democratic convention that offered him the nomination, which he intended to accept. But party leaders were not interested in bringing a president as unpopular and handicapped as Wilson had become back into the political arena to run for an unprecedented third term, which he was sure to be denied. Instead, the Democrats turned to James Cox, a progressive governor from Ohio.

The Republicans, convinced that the country was tired of progressive appeals for domestic change and grand world designs, moral sacrifice and reform, nominated Ohio senator Warren G. Harding. Wilson had it right when he asked, "How can he lead when he does not know where he is going?" H. L. Mencken, the *Baltimore Sun* journalist and pundit with a razor-sharp pen, said of Harding: He is a "blank cartridge." Mencken castigated Harding's "speechifying": "It reminds me of a string of wet sponges; it reminds me of tattered washing on the line; it reminds me of stale bean soup, of college yells, of dogs barking idiotically through endless nights. It is so bad that a sort of grandeur creeps into it. . . . It is rumble and bumble. . . . It is balder and dash." And then, most tellingly, he added, "As democracy is perfected, the office [of president] represents, more and more closely, the soul of the people. We move toward a lofty ideal. On some great and glorious day the plain folks of the land will reach their heart's desire at last, and the White House will be adorned by a downright moron." He expected Harding to serve for four or perhaps even eight years—"a ruler with the high ideals of a lodge joiner and the general intellectual lift and punch of a mackerel." William G. McAdoo, Wilson's son-in-law and Treasury secretary, famously declared that a Harding campaign speech put him in mind of "an army of pompous phrases moving over the landscape in search of an idea. Sometimes these meandering words actually capture a straggling thought and bear it triumphantly, a prisoner in their midst, until it died of servitude and over work."

A perfect fit for the national mood, Harding rode to victory on a theme of "Americanism." Asked what the term meant, Pennsylvania Republican boss Boies Penrose replied, "Damned if I know, but you can be sure it's going to get a lot of votes." He was right: Harding won 60 percent of the popular vote and a landslide in the Electoral College; it was one of the greatest victories in presidential history. "It wasn't a landslide," Wilson's press secretary Joe Tumulty said. "It was an earthquake."

Although Harding was no world-beater as president (he is remembered now as little better than James Buchanan, generally seen as the worst president in American history), Harding enjoyed considerable popularity with the press and public. He cultivated reporters and endeared himself to voters by refusing to mount ad hominem attacks on Wilson, saying, "I will never go to the White House over the broken body of Woodrow Wilson." Nor would he publicly criticize his Democratic opponent James Cox for being divorced and remarried. He died in office in 1923 before the Teapot Dome scandal would become seen as one of the worst scandals in presidential history and play havoc with Harding's contemporary standing.[10]

For all Wilson's accomplishments and high-minded idealism, he left behind a history of misleading or overstated presidential promises that added to TR's arbitrary use of presidential power to make future politicians less than truthful about their intentions and actions, and left voters cynical about trusting anyone running for the White House. Still, Wilson is remembered to this day as a great visionary. True, he did not achieve his lofty ambitions for a democratic world or an end to wars, but he set a standard that encouraged future presidents to identify their administrations with some advance toward a great or greater America. Even presidents who recalled little about Wilson's two terms have been influenced by the idea of identifying themselves with soaring aspirations and winning a memorable place in the country's history.

Yet Wilson's deception of the public about his capacity to conduct presidential business set a precedent for future leaders to be less than aboveboard about their actions. Just as Wilson's deceit has cast a shadow over his historical reputation, so future presidential deceptions have made Americans cynical about politicians, and have undermined our democracy.

CHAPTER 3

Franklin D. Roosevelt

Prophet of a New Order

=====

After Franklin Roosevelt died in office in April 1945, the twelfth year of his presidency, the *New York Times*, never a consistent supporter, declared that a hundred years from now men would fall on their knees and thank the heavens that Franklin Roosevelt had been in the White House. Roosevelt was no saint, as a host of critics asserted, nor have I ever come across one in politics. Yet as most U.S. historians would agree, Roosevelt was one of three great American presidents along with George Washington and Abraham Lincoln.

Roosevelt's administration went far to restore hope in the country's economic and political systems and largely unified the nation, especially in the Second World War. His promise in 1932 of a New Deal and his urging that Democrats "be prophets of a new order" resonated forcefully with the public. This is not to suggest that he enjoyed unqualified support through his twelve plus years in office. No president, however popular, ever does; debate and dissent are the lifeblood of democracy. Yet Roosevelt went below 50 percent approval in the Gallup polls only once.

When Roosevelt entered the Oval Office in 1933, the country had been through a decade of constant division. A split between urban modernists and rural fundamentalists, especially across the South, had distinguished the twenties. Prohibition under the Eighteenth Amendment to the Constitution; anti-immigration sentiments driving the National Origins Act of 1924; the prominence of the anti-black, anti-Catholic, anti-Semitic Ku Klux Klan in rural communities across the country; the anti-evolution movement making headlines through the John T. Scopes trial in Dayton, Tennessee, in 1925; and the Sacco-Vanzetti murder convictions in Massachusetts in 1927 reflected the resentment of rural America to the shift of power to big cities crowded with immigrants who held different values.

Between 1929 and 1933, when the country fell into the worst economic crisis in its history, divisions in the country deepened. Antagonism to corporate America and especially to Herbert Hoover's business administration expressed itself in descriptions of shantytowns, retreats of the unemployed and homeless, as "Hoovervilles," amid complaints that bankers and munitions makers driven by profits and indifferent to human suffering had led the country into World War I. Democratic republicanism seemed on the verge of collapse, and many Americans looked to authoritarian regimes in Mussolini's fascist Italy, Hitler's Nazi Germany, and Stalin's communist Russia as models of what might replace capitalism and representative government in the United States. At the other extreme, administration opponents in the American Liberty League, founded in 1934, complained that Roosevelt, like European dictators, wanted unprecedented power to control the country. As FDR's administration embarked on its ambitious programs to remake the U.S. economy, these critics grew louder. His proposal to pack the Supreme Court in 1937 and to reorganize the executive branch in 1938 sparked heightened talk of the president's authoritarian tendencies. Nor did his eventual evacuation of 110,000 Japanese Americans (65 percent of whom were citizens) from the West Coast during World War II, later criticized by the Supreme Court as the greatest breach of civil liberties in American history, demonstrate his unqualified commitment to democratic principles. The evacuees suffered material loss and physical and emotional discomfort, especially the children, who carried the scars of their experience through the rest of their lives.

Roosevelt's greatest downturn in popular support came in 1937–38 when he proposed Supreme Court reform and the national economy fell into a recession. The Gallup polls in those two years reflected the erosion of his appeal when 68 percent of the public opposed his court-packing proposal, 72 percent favored anti-lynching legislation that Roosevelt resisted, 58 percent of the country blamed the business turndown on the administration, 64 percent said they were less well off than they were a year before, and 66 percent said they would vote against a woman for president, suggesting that Eleanor Roosevelt would have little chance of replacing her husband. Yet despite these Gallup polls, FDR never went below 54 percent approval in these two years and usually had between 55 and 60 percent favorable ratings. (What a contrast to Donald Trump, who has never reached 50 percent approval.)[1]

Through all the ups and downs of his presidency, Roosevelt never thought of becoming a dictator or of abandoning capitalism for socialism. In 1933, when Eleanor Roosevelt said that the country might benefit from a benevolent dictator "who could force through reforms," Franklin replied, "One could not count on a dictator staying benevolent." When the influential columnist Walter Lippmann suggested expanding presidential powers at the expense of Congress, Roosevelt asked Harvard law professor Felix Frankfurter to discourage

Lippmann from suggesting so radical a reform. Frankfurter told Lippmann that such talk could advance the rise of fascism in America. As historian Eric Rauchway has written, "Anti-fascism characterized both Roosevelt's New Deal, which was an effort to strengthen American democracy against fascist tendencies at home, and his foreign policy, which was an effort first to prevent the spread of, and then to defeat altogether, fascism abroad." Roosevelt's declaration of the "Four Freedoms" in 1941—freedom of speech and religion and freedom from want and fear—were hallmarks of his commitment to democracy.[2]

At the same time, he understood that the economic catastrophe challenged the country's traditional democratic institutions. He was also mindful of how national and international conditions gave demagogues like Louisiana's Huey Long and Father Charles Coughlin, the Detroit radio priest, unprecedented appeal in the United States. Both offered simplistic solutions to the Depression: Long promised to "Share Our Wealth" and "make every man a king" by redistributing the country's riches through confiscatory taxes on affluent Americans, and Coughlin proposed restoring prosperity by inflating the currency with silver-backed dollars—a populist nostrum first advanced in the late nineteenth century. Both men's personal dramatics excited audiences, including attacks on scapegoats such as corporations, Catholics, and Jews. Long was a brilliant exhibitionist whose "red hair, cherubic face, and pug nose" joined with flamboyant dress of "pongee suits . . . orchid colored shirts . . . striped straw hats, watermelon pink ties, and brown and white sports shoes" to make an indelible impression wherever he went, while Coughlin mesmerized radio audiences with promises of helping poor Americans by bringing down international bankers and Jews. As Huey Long's brother, Julius, said of Huey, "The only sincerity there was in him was for himself."[3]

All candidates for the presidency, having endured verbally abusive campaigns, end up with some angry feelings toward opponents, but follow a decorum that discourages public expression of their most virulent hostility. In 1944, for example, when Roosevelt ran against New York governor Thomas Dewey, he hid his strongest feelings, privately calling him a "son of a bitch." As recently as the 1970s, Richard Nixon, as recorded on his secret tapes, vented his frustration toward critics and competitors with anti-Semitic comments and descriptions of journalists as "cocksuckers." Yet he would never say such things in public.

In Roosevelt's day, such nastiness was largely set aside, because there was a sense of shared national distress. And Roosevelt worked hard to tame these divisions, which temporarily faded under his skillful direction despite the Long and Coughlin appeals to class war. Neither man could match Roosevelt's charisma and the appeal of his New Deal. His thirty "fireside chat" radio talks over twelve years resonated powerfully with millions across the country, and were a prelude to how John Kennedy and subsequent politicians would use television to appeal directly to Americans.

The economic crisis affected all Americans and broke down barriers between urban and rural populations. The economic collapse hit farmers and industrial workers alike. Young women working in textile mills in New England, for example, were earning seven and a half cents an hour and were thankful for the work. People in rural communities subsisted on one dollar a day before the New Deal gave them a safety net. The "Okies," from Oklahoma and surrounding states in the Southwest known as the Dust Bowl, fled their homes for California and other West Coast states in hope of a better life. It reminded folks of the wagon trains moving across the country in the nineteenth century. Some of them, exhausted by the futile pursuit of a new beginning, trekked back East in their covered wagons with messages scrawled on the sides such as "In God We Trusted! In Kansas We Busted!"

Like the shared suffering of the economic collapse, Roosevelt's New Deal was a unifying force, providing programs to help people in every part of the United States; his relief measures reduced misery across all regions and among all populations, including African Americans, even though Roosevelt never singled them out for help in deference to his racist southern supporters, though they were excluded from some of Roosevelt's domestic programs. The New Deal's alphabet agencies aided millions and helped humanize the country's industrial system.

The Federal Emergency Relief Administration (FERA) provided desperately needed aid to the most needy; the Civilian Conservation Corps (CCC) sent young men into the parks and woods to help conserve America's natural resources and provide their families with some badly needed cash; the Public Works Administration (PWA) refurbished the country's infrastructure with projects that provided jobs to millions of the unemployed; the Works Progress Administration (WPA) aided unskilled labor as well as artists, actors, musicians, and writers with grants; the Securities and Exchange Commission (SEC) regulated the bond and stock markets by protecting investors against fraud; the Federal Deposit Insurance Corporation (FDIC) initially guaranteed bank accounts up to $2,500 (today $250,000); the Home Owners Loan Corporation (HOLC) arranged refinancing of mortgages so that unemployed Americans would not lose their homes; the Agricultural Adjustment Administration (AAA) brought production into line with demand and raised prices on produce by paying farmers to destroy crops; the National Recovery Administration (NRA) similarly promoted management of output in order to raise prices and create jobs; and so much more was achieved by introducing unemployment insurance; Social Security protected the elderly from impoverishment; the National Labor Relations Act (NLRA) legitimized labor unions; the minimum wage and maximum hours law promoted decent working conditions; and the National Youth Administration (NYA) helped those between the ages of sixteen and twenty-five to stay in school and develop job skills.

These agencies were not a cure-all. The New Deal did not end the Depression, though it certainly helped ease the suffering. It expanded the TR and Wilson initiatives in establishing a welfare state that subsequent, more conservative presidents like Eisenhower and Reagan could not dismantle except at great political risk.

Roosevelt broke barriers in staffing his administration. He invited Catholics and Jews to serve prominent roles in his government, including Ben Cohen in his brain trust; Henry Morgenthau as secretary of the Treasury, the first Jew to serve in that post; Joseph Kennedy, the first Irish American to become ambassador to Great Britain; and Secretary of Labor Frances Perkins, the first female cabinet member. Roosevelt appointed fifty Catholics to serve on the federal judiciary, about six times the number named in the 1920s.

At the same time, however, Roosevelt resisted pressure to identify his White House with African Americans by failing to support anti-lynching legislation proposed by civil libertarians and opposed by southern segregationists. Only in 1938, when he turned against conservative southern Democrats in state primaries, did Roosevelt mount a campaign to oust them and liberalize the Democratic Party. In spite of his timidity in opposing southern bias, African Americans, helped by the New Deal's welfare measures, abandoned the Republican Party for Roosevelt and the Democrats, following injunctions to turn Lincoln's face to the wall.

Roosevelt presided over a stable government with limited personnel changes. He was masterful at disarming private grievances that arose between him and members of his administration. In 1932, for example, General Douglas MacArthur ousted the Bonus Army of World War I veterans from Anacostia Flats outside of Washington, D.C. The veterans were demanding bonuses promised to them, and Roosevelt saw MacArthur's actions as those of a man on horseback or "a potential Mussolini." Yet in 1933, when Roosevelt planned to transfer scarce funds from the country's small army of 140,000 men to a relief agency, MacArthur told Roosevelt, "When we lost the next war, and an American boy, lying in the mud with an enemy bayonet through his belly . . . spat out his last curse, I wanted the name not to be MacArthur but Roosevelt." Roosevelt angrily responded, "You must not talk that way to the President." MacArthur offered to resign. But Roosevelt, always eager to hide internal controversies from the public, responded by urging that they work out their differences and a compromise budget, which they did.

He feared public administration quarrels would signal a dysfunctional White House without the ability to be effective or command popular support. Roosevelt's emphasis on administrative stability was reflected in the fact that cabinet members Cordell Hull, Harold Ickes, Henry Morgenthau, and Frances Perkins served for most, if not all, of Roosevelt's twelve years.

While Roosevelt understood that any foreign policy initiative would always generate some criticism, he believed that the success of any major step in international relations depended on a stable national consensus that would not collapse if it fell short of promised goals. His appointments in 1940 of Republicans Henry Stimson and Frank Knox as secretaries of war and the navy, respectively, reflected his reach for bipartisanship in response to the European crisis. He believed Wilson's failure to achieve his postwar aim of joining the League of Nations and making the world safe for democracy partly stemmed from a domestic setback—the Republican victory in regaining control of the U.S. Senate in 1918. It demonstrated Wilson's loss of political support for his groundbreaking postwar program. Whether it would have worked was a different matter.

Roosevelt was determined to prevent domestic political differences from undermining his own foreign policy aims. Hence, in 1935, when Congress passed a neutrality law that barred loans to belligerents and forbade American citizens to travel on ships in war zones in any future conflict, he reluctantly signed a bill that was designed to prevent the same conditions that drew us into World War I; his opposition rested on the fact that it chiefly deprived the president of power to punish aggressor nations. Because it enjoyed widespread national support, vetoing it would have undermined his popularity, been decisive in weakening his ability to advance domestic economic recovery, and possibly threatened his reelection in 1936.

In the meantime, he was able to use the 1935 law to support his foreign policy and domestic political goals. When Italy attacked Ethiopia in East Africa as an initial step in reconstructing a Roman empire, Roosevelt invoked the 1935 neutrality law, forbidding loans to belligerents or travel on their ships in war zones. It was a ploy to punish Italy. After all, the only belligerent likely to ask for bank loans was Italy, and American travelers would boycott only Italian liners, which were in no jeopardy from mythical Ethiopian submarines. Roosevelt's actions put him squarely in line with American public opinion, which had little, if any, sympathy for Mussolini's assault on an undeveloped East African country.

Roosevelt's response to Rome's attack sat well with American voters as he faced the challenge of reelection. Moreover, in 1936, when a civil war erupted in Spain between Francisco Franco's fascists and the democratically elected Republican government, Roosevelt signed on to a second neutrality law, barring U.S. involvement in the conflict. While Roosevelt would later acknowledge that it was a mistake to stand aside in a civil war in which the United States could have legitimately provided arms and money to the existing democratic government of Spain, which was under siege from insurgents aided by fascist Italy and Nazi Germany, his neutrality stance strengthened his political position in the United States.

Roosevelt's campaign for reelection was a model of how to command a large national majority. His New Deal programs had created a wide base of support from Americans who saw him and his administration as dedicated to ending the Depression. He reminded voters of how far the country had come since the failed Hoover presidency, declaring in a memorable speech that the earlier "Government by organized money" was "unanimous in their hate for me—and I welcome their hatred. I should like to have it said of my administration that in it the forces of selfishness and of lust for power met their match. I should like to have it said of my second administration that in it these forces met their master."

Foreign affairs took center stage in his campaign as well. In August, at Chautauqua, New York, a storied convention site, Roosevelt assured the country that under his leadership America would not go to war or allow itself to become involved in conflicts abroad. In memorable lines, he declared, "I have seen war. . . . I have seen blood running from the wounded. I have seen men coughing out their gassed lungs. I have seen the dead in the mud. I have seen cities destroyed. . . . I have seen children starving. I have seen the agony of mothers and wives. I hate war. . . . I shall pass unnumbered hours, thinking and planning how war may be kept from this nation." It was a speech calculated to win votes at home rather than influence events abroad.

The result of the 1936 election was overwhelming. Roosevelt won forty-six of the forty-eight states, enjoying a riff on the old saying, "As Maine goes, so goes the nation," changed to "As Maine goes, so goes Vermont." And Roosevelt captured over 60 percent of the popular vote against Republican Alf Landon, governor of Kansas, in one of the great landslides in presidential history, and the Democrats commanded supermajorities in both houses of Congress.

For all Roosevelt's pacifist and isolationist talk during the 1936 campaign, he immediately followed his victory with a goodwill trip to Buenos Aires, Argentina. It was a way of not only cementing his Good Neighbor policy with the southern republics but also a signal to Italy, Germany, and Japan, the world's principal antidemocratic combative nations, that the United States would not be indifferent to acts of aggression. The three bandit nations, as Roosevelt called them, had already put the democracies on notice of their intentions with their attacks in China and Africa, and with Germany's overt moves to reoccupy and rearm the Rhineland and build an air force.

In an October speech in Chicago, a center of Midwest isolationism, Roosevelt urged a quarantine of aggressors. Warning that international law and morality were at stake in discouraging attacks on weaker nations, Roosevelt predicted that the epidemic of lawlessness could spread to the Western Hemisphere and threaten the United States. He hoped his speech would stand as "a warning to the nations that today are running amuck" and make Americans more mindful of what was happening abroad. Instead, the speech increased isolationist warnings against letting Roosevelt drag us into another war.

In 1938, Hitler's annexation of Austria, the Anschluss, and his

threats of action against Czechoslovakia over the Sudetenland triggered European war fears. The British and French resolved them by
giving in to Hitler's demands at a Munich conference in September.
Although British prime minster Neville Chamberlain won international acclaim by declaring "peace in our time," Winston Churchill
is said to have declared, "The Prime Minister had a choice between
humiliation and war. He chose humiliation and now he will have
war." Roosevelt initially chimed in with a telegram to Chamberlain saying, "Good Man!" But like Churchill, he saw nothing good
coming from Chamberlain's appeasement of the German dictator.
In November, Roosevelt told his military chiefs to start manufactur-
ing fifteen thousand warplanes a year—not in preparation for U.S.
involvement in a war, but for sale to London and Paris to meet the
German threat.

Germany's annexation of the rest of Czechoslovakia in March 1939
convinced the British and French governments that Hitler could no
longer be trusted. Threats to Poland, which had won guarantees of
British and French support, brought Europe once again to the brink
of war. Because Roosevelt believed that a war was coming and was
eager to help the democracies against the Nazis, he asked the Senate
Foreign Relations Committee to sponsor a revised neutrality law providing for "cash and carry," meaning that London and Paris could
buy U.S. arms if they paid cash and carried them away in their own
ships. Unlike World War I, there would be no war debts or American
lives at risk from German submarines. The refusal of William Borah
of Idaho, a staunch isolationist and member of the Senate Foreign Relations Committee, to support the president's proposal, saying there
would be no war, angered Roosevelt and Secretary of State Cordell
Hull. When the war broke out in September with Germany's invasion of Poland, the administration had a Pyrrhic victory.

With the passage of a revised neutrality statute in November, Roosevelt temporarily found a way to support the democracies, but his satisfaction was short-lived. Fearful that Hitler's quick conquest of Poland would bring a spring offensive in the West, Roosevelt sent Sumner Welles, his undersecretary of state, on a peace mission to Europe in hope of delaying new German advances. But none of the belligerents were interested in talks. Consequently, in the spring, Nazi armies conquered Denmark, Norway, the Netherlands, Belgium, and, shockingly, France, with 330,000 British and French troops compelled to evacuate the continent at Dunkirk in northern France in early June.

The French collapse and potential German invasion and defeat of Great Britain sent a shock wave through the United States and persuaded Roosevelt to run for a third term. As important, it allowed Roosevelt to trade fifty overage American destroyers for ninety-nine-year leases on British bases in the Atlantic and Caribbean approaches to the United States. Instead of persuading Americans that the president had reduced the country's defensive power, it was celebrated as the greatest deal for the United States since the Louisiana Purchase of 1803. In addition, Roosevelt was able to convince Congress and the country that it needed an unprecedented peacetime draft. The law promised to release the men after one year of training and to limit their deployment to the Western Hemisphere. What gave the army buildup backing was the woeful state of the country's military preparedness, underscored by stories of army units using broomsticks as rifles and milk trucks as tanks in combating a make-believe invasion of the United States.

In the 1940 election, Roosevelt repeatedly promised that the country would not go to war unless attacked by a foreign power. That was his consistent message until the end of October when, with polls showing steady American opposition to involvement in the fighting; and Wendell Willkie, his Republican opponent, declaring the boys were already all but on the transports, Roosevelt made a blanket promise not to enter the war, omitting the qualifier "unless attacked by a foreign power." It opened Roosevelt to later charges that the Pearl Harbor attack was no surprise and served as a back door to the European war he always intended to fight.

When Roosevelt won reelection in November and Churchill advised him that Britain was broke and could no longer pay cash for war supplies, Roosevelt came up with lend-lease, a way to keep supplying the British while the Germans mounted an aerial assault on the British Isles that threatened to defeat them. While the great majority of Americans favored Britain in the war, they remained opposed to belligerency. But settled in his third term with no election on the horizon, Roosevelt moved closer to direct involvement in the fighting by authorizing the convoying of American supply ships into war zones. Still, his control of foreign affairs remained precarious. After agreeing to supply Moscow with lend-lease goods when Hitler invaded Russia in June 1941, Roosevelt came within one vote of losing the peacetime draft in the lower house.

The Japanese solved Roosevelt's dilemma of how to help defeat the Axis powers when they staged a surprise attack on Pearl Harbor in Hawaii on December 7, 1941, and Germany and Italy declared war on the United States on December 11. Once in the war, Roosevelt had two compelling goals: to defeat the Axis powers and to bring the country through the fighting ready to accept an end to isolationism and a postwar part in international affairs.

Both aims required skillful management of a host of domestic political crosscurrents. Because public opinion wanted principally to strike back against Japan first, and Moscow urged a quick second front in the West to ease the pressure on Soviet forces fighting for their lives, Roosevelt had to find ways to satisfy or at least partly meet these conflicting demands. American domestic opinion received assurances of Pacific and East Asian action by sending General Joseph "Vinegar Joe" Stilwell to command American and Chinese forces in China, Burma, and India. At the same time, the incarceration of Japanese-Americans in the United States gave Americans the feeling that we were fighting back. This was heightened when Colonel James Doolittle and a squadron of redesigned bombers flying off of aircraft carriers struck Tokyo, followed by naval victories in 1942 in the Coral Sea and at Midway Island.

To meet Stalin's demand for prompt action in the West, Roosevelt told Soviet foreign minister Vyacheslav Molotov in May that the U.S. and Britain would open a second front in the fall of 1942, which he knew insufficient trained forces and inadequate landing ships put out of reach. Yet he hoped it would temporarily boost Soviet morale. Although chief of staff General Dwight D. Eisenhower opposed it as a strategic error, an invasion of North Africa coupled with day/night bombing raids on German cities went far to put Stalin's demands on hold. An Anglo-American promise at a Casablanca conference in January 1943 to insist on unconditional surrender by all the Axis powers was another attempt to convince Moscow that Churchill and Roosevelt had every intention of inflicting a decisive defeat on Mussolini, Hitler, and Hideki Tojo, Japan's war leader. An invasion of Sicily and Italy that triggered Mussolini's demise later that year, followed by the massive D-Day invasion of France at the Normandy beaches in June 1944, led to the collapse of Hitler's Germany and victory in Europe that Churchill and Roosevelt had aimed to achieve first.

The defeat of Nazism did not come soon enough to save the lives of six million European Jews who perished in Hitler's concentration camps. Roosevelt's historical reputation has suffered under the ret-rospective understanding that while he promised to punish war criminals for their various crimes, which later became the basis for war crime trials in Nuremberg, Germany, his interest in deterring the killings with relaxed immigration laws fell before State Depart-ment preference for rescue through victory rather than air attacks on rail lines and crematoria in Auschwitz, Poland. Roosevelt was more responsive to anti-Semitic and anti-immigration sentiment in the United States than the urgency of saving Europe's Jews. His last-minute decision in 1944 to set up a War Refugee Board that saved some thirty thousand Jews from the death camps was as much the product of concern about losing the Jewish vote in New York in the 1944 election as a commitment to saving Hitler's victims.

While Roosevelt's top priority was military victory, he also gave consistent support to promoting internationalism. And here he was as devious as Theodore Roosevelt had been in making national secu-rity appear to be American altruism, though it was also the product of idealism. Roosevelt fully appreciated that if the country was going to shift to internationalism, it would need to believe that this was the war to end all wars, and a world made safe for democracy with a new world league that punished aggressors, defended peace, and pro-moted his Four Freedoms and the ideals of the August 1941 Atlantic Charter that celebrated democratic values. When he met with Stalin and Churchill at Yalta in the Soviet Crimea in February 1945, he won a paper commitment to a declaration on Eastern Europe prom-ising that countries liberated from Nazi control would enjoy the self-determination Wilson had described in his Fourteen Points.

Winning American opinion to support high ideals was the least of Roosevelt's challenges in moving the country to internationalism. The greater obstacle was to convince a majority that England, France,

China, and Russia would follow our lead in reforming international affairs. For one, trust in British adherence to anti-colonialism was in short supply, despite the American public's infatuation with Churchill. And the picture of a stable postwar great-power China was not easy to arrange. Roosevelt understood that America's view of a reliable Chinese ally helping police Asia was more fiction than reality. But because China was the country's favorite wartime ally and a vital part of American hopes for the postwar world, Roosevelt did all he could to promote the public's romance with China. When Madame Chiang Kai-shek came to the United States in the winter of 1942–43 and Congress and the press swooned over her, Roosevelt felt compelled to treat her like royalty. Behind the scenes, however, it was a different story. When he told a press conference that we will send supplies to China just as fast as the good Lord will allow, she embarrassed him by saying, "I understand you have a saying in your country that the Lord helps those who help themselves." Roosevelt turned beet red with anger, and when he returned to the White House, he told Treasury secretary Morgenthau, who had financial dealings with the nationalist government, "Get that bitch out of here."

In 1944, when Roosevelt sent a new ambassador to Chiang's government in Chunking, the wartime capital, he selected Patrick Hurley, a conservative Republican, Oklahoma businessman, and Herbert Hoover's secretary of war. It was a political maneuver: Hurley knew nothing about China (he addressed Chiang Kai-shek as Mr. Shek). Roosevelt instructed Hurley to negotiate a coalition government between the Nationalists and the Communists. If it failed and China erupted into postwar civil strife, Roosevelt expected to blame it on the Republican Hurley. Roosevelt was determined to keep the illusion of a stable, cooperative China in the service of advancing American involvements abroad.

For Roosevelt, Russia was the key to convincing American opinion that postwar relations would be a lovefest among victorious allies. Roosevelt's references to Stalin and the Russian people during the war strengthened the hope for postwar cooperation. After coming back from a Tehran conference in December 1943, Roosevelt said in a fireside chat that he had "got along fine with Marshall Stalin . . . I believe he is truly representative of the heart and soul of Russia; and I believe we are going to get along very well with him and the Russian people—very well indeed." At a subsequent news conference about future relations with Moscow and his impressions of Stalin, he told reporters, "We had many excellent talks" which would "make for excellent relations in the future." Reporters, who remained doubtful, asked the president what type of man he was: "Is he dour?" Roosevelt replied, "I would call him something like me . . . a realist."

But behind the public rhetoric of optimism were Roosevelt's private convictions that the world remained volatile and drawn to conflict. And he had doubts about Soviet commitment to a postwar league. He also wondered whether the American public would remain steadfast in its willingness to join a world organization and take responsibility for overseas affairs. He told Edward R. Stettinius, his undersecretary of state, that the issue he saw ahead was not whether the U.S. could make the world safe for democracy but whether democracy could make the world safe from another war.

Because he had serious concerns about postwar Soviet cooperation and willingness to follow through on agreements for self-determination among East European countries bordering Russia, and about continuing Soviet interest in world revolution, Roosevelt wanted a counterforce to its large standing armies. He saw it in exclusive control of unprecedentedly powerful atomic bombs that the United States and Britain were rushing to construct before Germany could build them. In the fall of 1944, he and Churchill signed an aide-mémoire to keep the development of nuclear power to themselves and not share atomic secrets with Moscow. These were not the actions of someone convinced that postwar relations with the Soviet Union would result in a cooperative world at peace.

It is worth repeating what Roosevelt told Orson Welles, the prominent screen personality: "Orson, you and I are the two greatest actors in America." Roosevelt's ability to take on a role or play a part served his political purposes, especially in disguising his inner thoughts on other countries and their leaders. Like his cousin Theodore, Franklin had a public face and a private one. In his dealings with Stalin and Russia, in particular, he promoted a fictional view of Stalin's eagerness for postwar friendship with the United States in order to assure that Americans would support a greatly expanded role in international affairs. We can assume that if he had lived to see the U.S.-Soviet falling out, he would have been quick to argue that he had tried hard to reach accommodation with Moscow, but that now we have to shift ground.

In the meantime, he felt compelled to promote hopes of a better world. His distortions about future international affairs were skillful, as was his ability to hide his disability and convince Americans that he had largely recovered from polio and could walk. And that in 1944, when he was in physical decline and dying, that he remained healthy enough to serve a fourth term—something voters wanted to believe as long as the war continued.

It would be awhile before a majority of Americans saw through Roosevelt's sleight of hand. And when they did, it increased their cynicism about all politicians and attraction to candidates for high office who were novices in the business of public service. It helped open the way to people who spoke against establishment politicos and promised a new day in political affairs. More important, Roosevelt's deceptions further encouraged future politicians to hide the truth. They imitated FDR in believing that they knew better than the public what was good for it and the country's future. Some of them were right, but they would have better served the national well-being if they had been more open and direct with the public about what they believed and how they were implementing their designs. In Roosevelt's case, his hidden actions generally served the country. At the end of the day, he set a standard for national change that is the envy of every future president, and a mark to aim for to be remembered as a groundbreaking leader.

CHAPTER 4

Harry S. Truman

The Tribulations of a Great President

———

In 1935, when Harry Truman entered the U.S. Senate as Missouri's junior senator, he was described as the senator from Pendergast, referring to the state's political boss, Thomas J. Pendergast. Truman's previous eight years as the presiding judge of Jackson County, which was tantamount to being the mayor of Kansas City, had also resulted from his ties to Pendergast's machine. During his Senate campaign, he was attacked as a "machine stooge" and Pendergast's "bell hop" or "errand boy." But unlike Pendergast, who was eventually sent to prison for tax fraud, Truman was a straight arrow who had served as a captain of artillery in World War I and would earn a reputation in the Senate as a hardworking, honest, unpretentious Democrat and consistent supporter of Roosevelt's New Deal.

In 1944, after Truman had chaired a Senate investigating subcommittee on fraudulent defense spending that made him something of a political star, including a *Time* magazine cover, he became a serious contender for FDR's fourth-term running mate. The decline of Roosevelt's health, which was obvious to close observers, triggered a hard-fought competition for the vice presidency. Henry Wallace, the sitting vice president, was Roosevelt's choice, but because southern conservatives threatened to split the Democratic convention and jeopardize Roosevelt's fourth-term election, the president agreed to take Harry Truman, who was considered the perfect party centrist. When Truman received the nomination, he was belittled as the second Missouri compromise, recalling the 1820 agreement that balanced the admission of slave-state Missouri to the Union by granting statehood to free-state Maine. Truman, at five feet nine and 175 pounds, was also dismissed as the little man from Missouri. In the long run, Truman's height was no disadvantage. But the public seems to like the idea of a president who is six feet and above.

Truman's eighty-two days as vice president were uneventful—largely because Roosevelt consulted him very little and never even told him about the work on an atomic bomb. The vice president was also kept in the dark about Roosevelt's February 1945 trip to Yalta, told only that the president was away and if absolutely necessary could be reached through the White House. Truman took all this in stride, assuming that his principal function as VP would be as a liaison between the Senate and the president. Given Roosevelt's precarious health, his limited contacts with his vice president were an egregious error, especially because Roosevelt privately talked about resigning after one year and heading an international peace organization. Perhaps Roosevelt thought that he could, in time, brief Truman on his future plans, or maybe he intended to serve out his full four-year term. We shall never know.

On April 12, at about five in the afternoon, Truman, who was having a drink with House Speaker Sam Rayburn, was summoned to the White House. When he arrived, he was met by Eleanor Roosevelt who told him that the president had died. After a brief stunned silence, he asked, "Is there anything I can do for you?" She famously replied, "Is there anything *we* can do for you? For you are the one in trouble now."

The exchange has always impressed me as a demonstration of how civilized people behave toward each other in times of grief and stress. Mrs. Roosevelt was a person of great compassion who sympathized with the struggles of underprivileged Americans, even when she herself was facing personal tragedy. Likewise, Harry Truman was known to fellow senators and White House officials as an affable man whom Allen Drury, a tough-minded journalist, described as "one of the finest men I know." The *New Republic*'s Richard Strout called him "a nice man, an honest man, a good Senator, a man of great humility and a man of courage." Yet no one was confident that he would measure up as a president, including Truman himself, who told reporters the next day that he felt as if "the moon, the stars and the planets had all fallen on me." Compounding the difficulty was the burden of following FDR, who after twelve years and two great national crises was already being considered one of the country's great presidents.

Yet Truman, whose modesty partly defined him, was not sold on Roosevelt's grandiosity. He complained to Bess Truman, his wife, reflecting on FDR's detachment from him, "He's so damn afraid that he won't have all the power and glory that he won't let his friends help as it should be done." Truman confided to Allen Drury about what happened when he met with the president. "He does all the talking, and he talks about what he wants to talk about, and he never talks about anything you want to talk about, so there isn't much you can do." It was Roosevelt's technique for holding visitors at bay or avoiding requests for anything he did not wish to give or, in Truman's case, keeping him on the sidelines.[1]

However modest Truman was, he was not without competitive instincts. He told Bess that winning was something that always animated him. For example, he approached his first major international meetings in the summer of 1945 with a mix of anxiety and determination to assert himself. In April 1945, when he saw Soviet foreign secretary Molotov at the White House, eleven days after Roosevelt died, he tried to make clear that he would insist on having Moscow honor its postwar commitments, especially on freedom for East European countries and Poland in particular. He said later that he gave Molotov "the one-two right to the jaw." When Molotov said that he had never been talked to that way before, Truman replied, "Honor your agreements and you won't be talked to that way again." Truman also understood the need at the time to keep so delicate an exchange private.

In July 1945, Truman was on edge about meeting with Churchill and Stalin at a conference in Potsdam, a suburb of Berlin. During the war, both men had become larger than life, like FDR; Truman felt dwarfed by them. But when he met with his two counterparts and found that he was a bit taller than either one of them, saying Stalin at five feet five was "a little bit of a squirt," he felt less intimidated. Moreover, he had told Churchill that he was fully informed about the late president's intentions and would be doing what FDR would have done. It was meant to tie Truman to Roosevelt's agenda and give him instant standing with the British and Soviet leaders. Truman found Churchill "charming" and "very clever," but dismissed his praise of Roosevelt and himself and America as "a lot of hooey." But he was sure they would get along "if he doesn't try to give me too much soft soap."

When Churchill lost a reelection bid as prime minister in the midst of the conference to Clement Attlee, the untested head of Britain's

Labour Party, it further bolstered Truman's confidence. Moreover, news of a successful test of the atomic bomb in the New Mexico desert gave Truman a stronger hand, or at least he thought so. But when he told Stalin about the United States' new powerful weapon, Stalin showed no concern. Having known about it from spies in the Manhattan Project, Stalin calmly responded that he hoped we would make use of it against the Japanese.

Indeed, Truman's most compelling duty was to end the war in Asia as soon as possible with the lowest cost to American lives. The decision to use the all-new powerful weapon against Japan to forestall an invasion of its home islands seemed entirely reasonable at the time. Because the United States is the only nation to have ever used nuclear bombs in combat, the decision has become controversial, with one argument being that Japan was already on the edge of surrender and the bomb was used instead to intimidate Moscow. But this was certainly not a prime consideration for Truman.

Two issues dominated Truman's thinking. First, that an invasion might cost the U.S. as much as a quarter of a million men or possibly more. Nobody of course could say with any assurance what the toll might be. But the fact that Japanese troops had so readily sacrificed themselves during the island-hopping campaigns, and that kamikaze fighters on suicide missions had readily crashed their planes into U.S. naval vessels, strengthened the conviction that the Japanese would defend their home islands without limits and raised the specter of a dreadful bloodbath. The U.S. had already lost some four hundred thousand troops in all the fighting, making these potential casualties especially chilling. Second, using a single plane to do what large formations had been doing to cities like Dresden in Germany and Tokyo in Japan made atomic bombings seem less costly. It is largely in retrospect, with the production of even more powerful hydrogen bombs, that the atomic attacks on Hiroshima and Nagasaki seem as apocalyptic as they now do.[2]

In the summer and fall of 1945, with 85 percent of Americans approving of Truman's decision to use the atomic bombs against Japan, the war coming to an end, and a majority of Americans endorsing a long-term occupation of Japan and believing that Russia could be trusted to cooperate with the United States, Truman enjoyed approval ratings in the eighties. By early 1946, however, as labor walkouts for pay increases in response to inflation roiled the national economy, and relations with the Soviet Union soured, the president's popularity began to sink: In January it had dropped to 63 percent; by April, with majorities saying that Russia aimed to dominate the world and would not cooperate with the United States, Truman was seen as less popular than Generals Douglas MacArthur and Dwight D. Eisenhower; by June, his disapproval rating was two points greater than his approval of only 43 percent; and by September, with 60 percent fearing another depression in the next ten years, and 71 percent opposing Russia's international behavior, only 32 percent of the country was positive about Truman. Shortly before the November elections, 71 percent of Americans said that they were having a harder time making economic ends meet than in the previous year. It was the worst sort of response a sitting administration could want in an election season.

The president was now ridiculed with the saying "To Err Is Truman." Allegations of communist subversion in the Roosevelt and Truman administrations on top of the pocketbook issues gave Republicans a clear advantage in the fall congressional elections. They mounted a campaign asking voters, "Had enough strikes? Had enough inflation? Had enough Communism?" Voters answered with a resounding yes. For the first time since 1930, the Republicans gained control of both houses of Congress. Democratic senator J. William Fulbright of Arkansas urged Truman to appoint a Republican secretary of state and then resign. With no vice president in place since Truman had replaced FDR in 1945, and no Twenty-Fifth Amendment to the Constitution establishing presidential authority to appoint a new VP, the Republican secretary would become the new president. In December 1946, Truman's approval stood at 35 percent, with 47 percent disapproving of his job performance.[3]

Yet Truman was not about to concede defeat. He said Fulbright should be called "half bright," and he laid plans to run in 1948, convinced that if he did his best for the national interest, he could persuade voters to give him a full term. By late January, with the 1946 midterm elections over, Truman saw a surge of public support. His approval rating jumped to 48 percent and his disapproval fell to 39 percent. Truman believed that if he were to make a mark in the next two years, it would have to be in foreign affairs; Republicans controlled domestic policy. In 1947, when Congress passed the antilabor Taft-Hartley law reining in unions, for example, Truman vetoed it. But congressional Republicans overrode his veto and resisted any new welfare state initiatives.

On one issue, however, Truman felt compelled to initiate domestic action in civil rights. His background from southern Missouri was no predicate for a reform agenda on equal treatment of the races. But incidents of attacks on returning black army veterans in Deep South states angered Truman, who wrote a friend, "The main difficulty with the South is that they are living eighty years behind the times and the sooner they come out of it the better it will be for the country and themselves." He saw something radically wrong with the system when unlawful attacks on blacks went unpunished. He was determined to do something about it, and it began with a 1948 Civil Rights

Commission report, *To Secure These Rights*. In response, Truman asked Congress for an anti-lynching law, voting rights for blacks, and an end to segregation in interstate travel.

Truman's civil rights initiatives did not sit well with the public: 56 percent told Gallup pollsters that they opposed its passage "as a whole." But Truman was prepared to take the consequences, writing his friend that if his actions meant his defeat in 1948, at least it would be on behalf of a good cause. He also intended his civil rights program as a response to criticisms of American racism that the Soviets promoted to people of color around the globe. In the emerging Cold War contest with communism, the United States could not afford to ignore the African, Asian, and Latin American peoples who were the targets of the Soviets' anti-American propaganda.[4]

With the Cold War heating up, Truman focused his leadership on the international communist threat. In 1946, he had sent General George C. Marshall, a man for whom he had unbounded respect, to China to arrange a truce in the Chinese civil war between Chiang Kai-shek's Nationalist government and Mao Tse-tung's Communist insurgents. But the two sides simply couldn't find common ground and Marshall's mission went nowhere. In 1947–48, the civil war remained unsettled and subsequent complaints about losing China to communism were muted, though pressure to rescue Chiang's armies became a refrain among conservatives in and out of Congress.

At the same time, because Republican accusations of subversives in the Roosevelt and now Truman administrations found a responsive audience in the United States, Truman issued an executive order mandating loyalty tests for federal employees. It was more of an exercise in paranoia and political gamesmanship than a genuine policy for defending the country's national security. As historian David McCullough later pointed out, during four years, three million federal employees were investigated. While "several thousand would resign" rather than be subjected to Civil Service Commission scrutiny and FBI prying into their lives, "only 212 would be dismissed as being of questionable loyalty. None would be indicted and no espionage would be found." But Truman's record here is hardly a positive feature of his presidency. Bowing to political pressure, he was not above craven political gestures, a striking contrast with his courage on civil rights, demonstrating that sometimes leaders do both brave and cynical things. In 1947, confronted by the collapse of British influence in the Near East and the threatened success of communist subversion in Greece and Turkey, Truman rallied the United States' resistance with the pronouncement in March of the Truman Doctrine. Because Truman's proposal to provide $250 million in aid to each of the two countries initiated unprecedented U.S. involvement in Near East affairs, Truman "scared the hell" out of Americans by defining the aid as part of a conflict between authoritarian communism and Western support for self-determination in countries considered vital to America's national security. If anything could push Congress and the country into following Truman's lead, it was an appeal to national self-preservation in a struggle with Soviet communism. After his Truman Doctrine speech, his approval jumped to 60 percent, and 79 percent of Democrats said they wanted Truman to run in 1948. Yet 53 percent of the country thought that the Republicans would win the presidency in the following year. In June, when George Marshall, who had become secretary of state, gave a commencement address at Harvard University, he proposed a $17 billion plan to bolster West European economies. The goal was to stabilize Europe's democracies against communist parties tied to the Soviet Union. While commanding less public attention than Truman's Doctrine, the Marshall Plan also won widespread public approval.[5]

Early in 1948, when a coup in Czechoslovakia put that country in Moscow's orbit, a majority of Americans voiced support for U.S. participation in a military alliance with Western Europe's democracies. As it would be the first defensive-offensive alliance in U.S. history, it represented a radical shift away from isolationism. And even though Truman was seen as standing up to the communist threat, it did not translate into national popularity. In public opinion polls in the first half of 1948, Truman's approval ratings had fallen to the mid-to-high thirties and the disapproval response hovered around 50 percent.[6]

Throughout the summer of 1948, New York governor Thomas Dewey held a double-digit lead over Truman in a November matchup. Making matters even more difficult, progressive Democrats had abandoned Truman to support former VP Henry Wallace in a third-party bid, and southern conservatives antagonistic to Truman's civil rights program bolted the Democrats to form the Dixiecrat Party with Governor Strom Thurmond of South Carolina as their presidential candidate. In September, despite the dissenting Democrats on the left and the right, Truman began to cut into Dewey's lead, reducing the gap to between 6 and 7.5 points. In a final Gallup poll on October 25, Dewey still held a five-point lead. But Truman was clearly gaining ground. Because Wallace's Progressive Party was seen as an anti-American arm of the Communists and the Dixiecrats as advocates of un-American racism and the last vestiges of the South's "lost cause," neither fringe group was able to mount a serious challenge to either Truman or Dewey.

And Truman now seized the initiative in the campaign by calling the Republican Congress into a special session to make good on legislative promises. When, as he anticipated, it adjourned without a record of accomplishment, he was able to mount a rallying cry against the Republican "do-nothing, good-for-nothing Congress." His campaign, which was described as a "whistle-stop" train tour of cities across the country, became a legendary form of political appeal that has never reoccurred. Speaking from the back of the train after pulling into various cities and towns across the United States during thirty-three days in September and October, Truman promised to "give 'em hell." The crowds picked up on his promise and shouted back at him, "Give 'em hell, Harry." He connected brilliantly with his audiences who saw him as a fighting underdog and man of the people, urging Americans not to forget what Roosevelt and the New Deal had done for them, and promising what he could do in the future with what he called a Fair Deal as opposed to the "do-nothing" Republican Congress. The contrast to the stiff, somewhat pompous Dewey became all to Truman's advantage. The joke caught on that with his manicured mustache, Dewey looked like the bridegroom on the wedding cake and that his detached arrogance made him the only man who could strut sitting down.

Closing the gap with Dewey in the final weekend of the election, Truman pulled off the greatest upset in presidential history. Almost no one thought Truman would win, including the pollsters, who were embarrassed by their misreading of the national political mood. Truman won 303 electoral votes and outdid Dewey by 2.2 million popular ballots. The memorable image of Truman's victory is him holding up a copy of the *Chicago Tribune*, a fiercely anti-Truman newspaper, with the premature headline, "Dewey Defeats Truman." As someone said, it was a man-size victory or *Truman's* triumph. Truman won, Sam Rayburn said, because "he is one of the folks. He smiles with them and not at them, laughs with them and not at them." The administration's response to the Berlin blockade with the airlift that defeated the communist attempt to starve the western part of the city and force the American, British, and French out also bolstered Truman's appeal as a strong and effective foreign policy leader.[7]

As with Woodrow Wilson, who had hoped his presidency could focus on domestic reforms rather than foreign affairs, international challenges overtook Truman's four years between 1949 and 1952. His Fair Deal program of federal aid to education, universal health insurance, a Fair Employment Practices Commission to promote nondiscrimination in hiring, and repeal of the Taft-Hartley law quickly took a backseat to the Cold War threats facing the United States. In 1949, Truman led America's democratic allies in Europe to join a military alliance—the North Atlantic Treaty Organization (NATO). Lord Ismay, the alliance's first secretary-general, said NATO's goal was "to keep the Russians out, the United States in, and the Germans down."

The diplomat George Kennan opposed the establishment of the alliance as certain to militarize the Cold War, which it did when the Soviets established the Warsaw Pact in 1955, a mutual defense agreement between Russia and its East European satellites. Kennan also opposed Truman's decision to build hydrogen bombs, arguing that these were not battlefield weapons, could only be used against civilians in urban centers, and would do nothing more than touch off an arms race with the Soviet Union. To those who argued that it could serve as a deterrent to acts of aggression, Kennan responded that America's stockpile of atomic bombs was ample to deter any attack. Besides, he accurately predicted, the Soviets would not risk devastation by launching an offensive. Instead, they would seek gains by subverting democratic regimes and replacing them with pro-communist governments allying themselves to Moscow. Hence, it was the Marshall Plan rather than any military pact that would make the difference in meeting the Soviet threat. In retrospect, the diplomat George

Kennan saw the dangers in building hydrogen bombs. And it's fair to conclude that Truman's decision touched off an arms race with Moscow. But it would have happened even if Truman resisted being the first to build H-bombs. The Soviets would have started building them as soon as they could, and then the U.S. would have followed quickly.

As Truman began his second term, free of complaints about being on anyone's coattails, the communist challenge seemed so compelling that it took center stage in his Inaugural Address on January 20, 1949: He promised to maintain the Marshall Plan, announced the founding of NATO, and proposed a program of aid to underdeveloped countries as a way to outdo communist prophecies of Third World prosperity under socialism.

Nonetheless, 1949 proved to be a trial by fire: Mao Tse-tung's Communist armies overwhelmed Chiang Kai-shek's Nationalists, driving them off the mainland to the island of Formosa. Although the State Department issued a white paper asserting that the Nationalist collapse was the product of its corruption and unpopularity (an accurate assessment), Truman administration critics blamed the "loss" on subversives with communist sympathies in the U.S. government. And a conspiracy myth about America's betrayal of an ally roiled the country. In September, more bad news agitated the White House and the nation: The Soviets had successfully detonated an atom bomb, ten years sooner than American intelligence had predicted.

Seizing upon these setbacks, Wisconsin senator Joseph McCarthy intensified national divisions with a speech in February 1950, saying, "The reason why we find ourselves in a position of impotency in international affairs is not because our only powerful potential enemy has sent men to invade our shores, but rather because of the traitorous actions of . . . the State Department . . . [which] is thoroughly infested with Communists." It was nonsense, but it gave millions of Americans the sense that we could save ourselves not by fighting a nuclear war with the Soviet Union or containing it but by rooting out these alleged traitors.

The disturbing news about communist subversion in the United States was largely blamed on Truman. He took this attack in stride, recognizing that as president, he would be blamed for things beyond his control. As he memorably put it, "The buck stops here." Dean Acheson, who became Truman's secretary of state at the start of his new term, said of the president that he was "free of the greatest vice in a leader, his ego never came between him and his job."[8]

In 1950, when a war broke out on the Korean Peninsula, it became the great preoccupation of the next two and half years remaining in Truman's term. America's withdrawal of troops from South Korea and an Acheson speech drawing a security line in northeast Asia that omitted South Korea became an inducement to the communist North to invade the South and bring it under its control. Kim Il-sung, the North's dictator supported by Moscow, persuaded Stalin to let him attack the South. Mao was more wary, fearful that the United States would try to help Seoul take over the North, putting an anti-communist force on China's border at the Yalu River. But convinced that the United States would not want to become involved in an Asian war, Stalin gave Kim a green light.

The attack startled U.S. officials, and Truman, who was away in Missouri, came rushing back to Washington. Held fast by the analogy of British-French appeasement of Hitler at Munich in 1938, Truman promptly decided to resist the North's aggression. Although he was confident that he could command majorities in both houses of Congress if he asked for a declaration of war on North Korea, he decided instead to declare his response a "police action" in cooperation with other U.N. countries. Truman's concern was that if he asked Congress for a declaration of war it could turn into a larger conflict with Moscow, which had supplied the Koreans with their arms and green-lit Pyongyang's aggression. Convinced that the U.S. could quickly defeat North Korean forces, Truman believed it wise to limit the fighting to a U.N.-supported "police force."

While members of Congress did not protest, Truman's initiative opened the way to a new form of executive war-making power and was a precedent for subsequent presidents to dominate external affairs. True, there was the history of U.S. gunboat diplomacy in the Caribbean and Central America to police the Western Hemisphere without specific congressional sanction. But sending land and air forces into combat in East Asia without formal congressional approval, as the Constitution required, opened a new chapter in U.S. foreign policy. At the same time, it quieted conservative protests against his administration as weak on combating communism. However much foreign policy decisions are the product of judgments about external affairs, domestic politics are never far behind. The lesson Franklin Roosevelt held close was the need for consensus in any overseas struggle costing blood and treasure. Truman understood the need for consensus as well, especially against the backdrop of complaints against him and Democrats of weak responses to communist aggression.

By September 1950, in less than three months, the U.S., South Korean, and U.N. forces had driven the North Koreans back above the thirty-eighth parallel. It immediately raised the question of whether the U.S. should aim to unify all of Korea under South Korea's pro-American government or be content with having rescued the South from communist aggression. General Douglas MacArthur, the commander of United States forces in Asia, urged an all-out effort to unify the peninsula under Western control, and 64 percent of a Gallup poll agreed.

Truman flew to Wake Island in the Pacific to discuss the question with MacArthur, of whom Truman was anything but an unqualified fan. As he flew to the meeting, he wrote in his diary, "On my way to meet God." He described the general as a "Prima Donna," a "Brass Hat," and a "bunco man." He had already crossed swords with MacArthur at the end of August when the general had given a speech to the Veterans of Foreign Wars (VFW) in which he had described the defense of Chiang's rump government on Formosa as essential to national security. Although it had angered Truman, he decided against dismissing him for insubordination.

During Truman's meeting with MacArthur on Wake, he asked the general if he thought the Chinese would intervene if we toppled the North Korean government. MacArthur saw little chance of a Chinese intervention despite signals that they would indeed enter the fighting if North Korea's communist government collapsed. If they did come in, MacArthur said, they would be defeated: "There would be the greatest slaughter." He also predicted that the boys would be home by Christmas. Having seen Chiang Kai-shek's poorly led armies in World War II, he mistakenly assumed that the communist troops in Mao's armies were no better.

He was wrong on all counts. After U.S. and South Korean forces crossed the thirty-eighth parallel and moved up to the Yalu River on the border between China and North Korea, a Chinese army of 260,000 men crossed into Korea and routed allied forces. MacArthur said, "We face an entirely new war," and began asking for retaliatory strikes against China, including the use of Nationalist troops on Formosa. Once again forces supporting South Korea were driven down the peninsula in an embarrassing retreat. The appointment of General Matthew Ridgway to lead coalition troops brought a re-surgence of allied fortunes and the successful return to the thirty-eighth parallel by the spring of 1951. Truman, wishing to confine the conflict to Korea and avoid a larger war with China and potentially Russia, tread cautiously. But MacArthur, who was criticized in the press for the strategic failure that had brought the Chinese into the fighting and the allies' retreat, openly complained about the refusal of Washington to give him the wherewithal to defeat China's offensive. Privately, he urged the administration to consider using atomic bombs against Chinese targets.

In April, after MacArthur once again challenged Truman's leadership by publicly advocating a wider war in Asia, Truman felt compelled to dismiss him. In January 1951, as coalition forces struggled in Korea, Truman's approval rating fell to 36 percent, and in a straw poll about possible candidates in the 1952 presidential election, Truman trailed Dwight Eisenhower by 59 to 28 percent. By the spring, despite the coalition's renewed gains in the fighting, Americans had soured on the war: 49 percent thought it was a mistake to have defended South Korea and 66 percent said they wished us to pull out as soon as possible. Moreover, 64 percent of Americans wanted Congress to have a future check on a president's freedom to send troops overseas.

By February 1951, Truman's approval rating had fallen to an all-time low of 26 percent, with much loss of his support due to his decision to dismiss MacArthur. David McCullough says, "The reaction was stupendous, and the outcry from the American people was shattering." In an appearance before Congress, MacArthur gave a memorable address that won thunderous approval, including a congressman who worshipfully declared, "We heard God speak here today, God in the flesh, the voice of God!" His increasing unpopularity, coupled with the adoption of the Twenty-Second Amendment to the Constitution on February 27, 1951, limiting a president to two terms, convinced Truman not to run again. The amendment specifically exempted him, but his regard for the country's democratic tradition persuaded him that he would be ignoring the people's wishes by trying to win another term. Besides, he was realistic enough to know that pulling off another upset as in 1948 was at best unlikely.

After considerable thought and private discussions about the 1952 presidential election, Truman urged Illinois governor Adlai Stevenson to accept the Democratic nomination. When Stevenson responded with reluctance to accept the honor and burden, Truman told him, "Adlai, if a knucklehead like me can be President and not do too badly, think what a really educated smart guy like you could do in the job." Stevenson appreciated that his association with Truman, who remained unpopular in the closing days of his presidency, would go a long way to defeat him, especially when pitted against someone as appealing as General Dwight Eisenhower, whose campaign button said it all: "I Like Ike." Eisenhower's victory over Stevenson in November 1952 did not please Truman. But, as with all past presidents, he gracefully accepted the defeat as democracy's temporary verdict on him and the Democrats.[9]

In a farewell address on January 15, Truman said, "I will once again be a plain, private citizen of this great Republic. That is as it should be. Inauguration Day will be a great demonstration of our democratic process." He acknowledged that when he became president he had grave doubts about his capacity to do the job: "When Franklin Roosevelt died, I felt there must be a million men better qualified than I, to take up the Presidential task. But the work was mine to do, and I had to do it. And I have tried to give it everything that was in me." He reflected on the decisions, large and small, every president has to make: "He can't pass the buck to anybody." To be sure, Truman emphasized the legitimate gains made during his presidency. But he demonstrated his modesty and honorable character by graciously calling on the people to support the new president. His speech was an expression of regard for tradition, by an honest, compassionate man. It also reflected what earlier and subsequent presidents said and did when they left the White House, regardless of whether they left in defeat, or by decision after one term (Calvin Coolidge), or simply at the end of eight years, as now mandated by the Constitution.

By 1972, when Truman passed away, he had given extensive interviews to the journalist Merle Miller, which he published in *Plain Speaking: An Oral Biography of Harry S. Truman*. The book is a treasure trove of Truman's views, with some quotes about political opponents. He called Joe McCarthy a "moral pygmy," a "coward," "a political gangster," "a no-good son of a bitch," and "a demagogue." He pilloried Eisenhower for failing during his presidential campaign to denounce McCarthy for attacking General Marshall. He said of General MacArthur, "I fired him because he wouldn't respect the authority of the President. . . . I didn't fire him because he was a dumb son of a bitch, although he was." As for Richard Nixon, he described him as "a liar . . . I don't think the son of a bitch knows the difference between telling the truth and lying." When Truman was asked if he thought Nixon had read the Constitution, he replied, "I don't know. But I'll tell you this. If he has, he doesn't understand it."

The passage of time has changed the public's assessment of Truman. His 32 percent approval rating when he left office in January 1953 is now a distant memory. In recent rankings of presidents, Truman has been assessed as high as sixth best among all forty-five presidents. Presidential ratings are a bit like the stock market: they go up and they go down. But because Truman's containment policy defeated the Soviet Union in the Cold War without a military conflict, he commands much greater respect today. Memories of his outspokenness or "plain speaking" also have enduring appeal, especially alongside several successors who suffer from what has been called a credibility gap. The same attributes that helped Truman defeat Thomas Dewey in 1948 also contribute to the public's enduring regard for his presidential performance. He is now remembered as an ordinary American who rose to the challenge not only of following Franklin Roosevelt, who had become a larger-than-life figure, but also of successfully leading the nation through very difficult times.[10]

Truman's legacy, however, is not simply a shining star that commands enduring praise. The least stellar attribute of his seven and a half years in office was his failure to ask congressional approval for a war declaration against North Korea in 1950. It facilitated the rise of an imperial presidency that resonates to this day in an executive office that shows limited deference to Congress in both domestic and foreign affairs and even in its power to investigate wrongdoing by other government agencies and individuals, including the president.

CHAPTER 5

Dwight D. Eisenhower

The General as Peacemaker

In 1952, the United States was locked in a stalemated war in Korea, the Soviet Union dominated east central Europe with satellite governments and threatened Western Europe with nuclear weapons, and China, with more than half a billion people, had become another communist state. Latin America, the Middle East, and much of Africa seemed vulnerable to the siren song of socialism, and Joseph McCarthy stirred fears of a domestic communist coup with allegations about subversives in the federal government, the media, and institutions of higher learning. Thus, the great majority of Americans were eager to see a proven patriot with military experience in the Oval Office.

Dwight D. Eisenhower was a storied American figure: A West Point graduate who served with Douglas MacArthur in the Philippines, headed the army's War Plans Division after the Japanese attack on Pearl Harbor, and commanded the successful invasion of North Africa in November 1942 and the Allied invasion of France in June 1944. After the war he became the president of Columbia University, but returned to the army in 1950 to organize and command NATO forces. Having turned down invitations from both parties to run for president in 1948, he accepted the Republican nomination in 1952 and went on to win a decisive victory over Illinois governor Adlai Stevenson. To maintain his standing as something of a nonpartisan American (he claimed he had never voted in a national election) and an ambivalent participant in the country's political wars, he chose California senator Richard Nixon, a fierce anti-communist Republican partisan, as his running mate to lead the fight against the Democrats.

Nixon became the voice of the campaign's hard-edged politics. He decried Stevenson as an "egghead" and a Ph.D. graduate of Secretary of State Dean Acheson's "cowardly college of Communist containment." Like Eisenhower, Nixon avoided any talk of Joe McCarthy and refused to defend General George C. Marshall against slanderous attacks. Nixon also exploited the critical mood toward Truman's White House with a shorthand description of its failings as K1C2: Korea, communism, and corruption, stirring voter concerns about the war, subversion, and allegations of Truman administration wrongdoing.

Two weeks before the election, Eisenhower issued a statement that clinched his victory. Understanding how frustrated Americans were with the deadlock in Korea, he announced that if elected he would "concentrate on the job of ending the Korean War" by traveling to the war zone. He gave no hint of how he would end the fighting, but voters trusted his abilities as a military chief and took his commitment to go to Korea as a way he would fulfill his promise. The sixteen years of Democratic rule, combined with the current frustration about national security and the overexpansion of federal authority, led Eisenhower to a landslide in which he defeated Stevenson by more than six million popular votes and swamped him in the Electoral College by 442 to 89.

The campaign had demonstrated that Eisenhower was a natural politician who instinctively understood how to win people's confidence and reduce personal conflicts. During World War II, he had effectively managed the clashing interests of wartime allies. In U.S. domestic politics he didn't wish to be seen as a liberal or a conservative, rather as an ordinary American who reflected the country's common values. As *New York Times* journalist Tom Wicker later said, "With his wide grin, worldwide fame, outstanding record, easygoing manner, and arms extended in the familiar V-for-Victory gesture, the war hero—whether in informal groups or speaking to huge crowds—proved a splendid, though inexperienced, campaigner, with what was history's most effective political slogan: 'I like Ike.'" Arthur Krock, Wicker's colleague at the *Times*, saw Eisenhower as a man with an "attractively pensive" smile, an "infectious" grin, and a "hearty" laugh. "He fairly radiates 'goodness,' simple faith and [his] honest background."

Such was the devotion of voters that when an Ike advocate rebuked Wicker for violating his journalistic canon of neutrality by supporting Stevenson in 1956 and Wicker responded by explaining that Ike's history of heart troubles made him unfit for a second term, the woman replied, "Young man, I would vote for Eisenhower if he were *dead!*"[1]

Eisenhower's entrance into the White House signaled not the end but at least the temporary halt or slowdown to the federal government's social welfare expansion. Because he brought a number of General Motors executives into his administration, including its president, Charles E. Wilson, detractors compared Ike's corporate presidency to Calvin Coolidge's midtwenties administration with its motto that "the business of America is business." Wilson made so many gaffes that opponents joked that he had invented the automatic transmission so that he would always have one foot free to stuff in his mouth. Adlai Stevenson declared that all the New Dealers had left Washington to make way for the car dealers. The secretaries of state, Treasury, agriculture, and commerce were all staunchly conservative Republicans. Yet Ike was no conservative ideologue. After listening to Sinclair Weeks, his commerce secretary, at cabinet meetings, he complained that his views were "illogical" and hoped that he would "become a little bit more aware of the world as it is today." The only Democrat in the administration was Secretary of Labor Martin Durkin, who had headed the plumbers division of the American Federation of Labor (AFL). The *New Republic* observed that the cabinet consisted of "eight millionaires and a plumber."

To signal that this administration would be sympathetic to business or private enterprise, Eisenhower tried to convert Franklin Roosevelt's Tennessee Valley Authority (TVA) into a private utility. But it proved an overreach, or what Harry Truman called "creeping McKinleyism." The best Eisenhower could do was to halt the expansion of federal power projects and favor private power companies: for example, selling the Hells Canyon utility on the Snake River, the largest of federal power projects in the West, to a private company. The problem with a utility like TVA, Ike said, was that it took "taxes [from] Massachusetts to provide cheap power in the TVA area to lure Massachusetts industry away." When the city of Memphis wanted to increase its electric power by expanding the TVA, Eisenhower rejected the request and instead agreed to a contract with the Dixon-Yates private utilities to build steam plants to satisfy Memphis's need for more electricity. When Memphis decided to build its own steam plant and charges of corrupt dealings against Dixon-Yates cast a shadow over the contract, Eisenhower canceled the agreement. He saw public power projects as too much like those in the Soviet Union to warrant their proliferation in the United States.[2]

Eisenhower fell short as well in trying to end farm subsidies that paid farmers to limit production, a program begun under the New Deal's Agricultural Adjustment Administration (AAA) in 1933 to raise farm prices. Eisenhower thought farm subsidies did more to make farmers dependent on the federal government than assure them of a prosperous future. But, as he saw with other New Deal programs, including Social Security, once in place they were close to impossible to take away. In fact, he understood that however much he favored free enterprise and a reduction in welfare programs, they were popular and should not only remain but also grow. He supported extending Social Security to the farm and domestic workers omitted from the 1935 law. Only workers in the fields of commerce and industry, about half of America's labor force, were original participants in the program. In 1958, Ike convinced Congress to amend the program to cover ten million additional workers.

In 1953, in recognition of the federal government's changing role in the country's social life, Eisenhower created a Department of Health, Education, and Welfare and appointed a woman, Oveta Culp Hobby of Texas, to head it. He was especially sympathetic to putting federal support behind educational institutions. In 1958, he signed into law the National Defense Education Act that provided federal help to improve American schools and promote postsecondary education, especially in the fields of science, engineering, and technology. Tying education to defense made the law more palatable to advocates of traditional local control of schools opposed to a federal bureaucracy shaping curricula. Southern representatives were fearful that national standards for schools would become a demand for racial integration. But Soviet advances in science and technology made scientific education a national priority in the United States. While rapid U.S. advances in various fields of technology, including space, would ease the sense of falling behind, new custom dictated that every president appoint a prominent scientist as a White House adviser.[3]

Although Eisenhower was no Keynesian who favored deficit spending and unbalanced budgets to combat recessions, neither was he a Hoover-like opponent of government spending. He understood that when a major recession hit the country as it did in 1957–58, he would be labeled "an unsympathetic, reactionary fossil" if he did nothing. By 1956 he had balanced the federal budget but had committed himself to buoying the economy with a federal highway program that eventually injected over $400 billion in federal funds into the national economy. Although the program was more a defense initiative than an economic one, he grasped that government spending had become a major instrument of national prosperity. Eisenhower said that periodically the federal government had to put a "floor over the pit of personal disaster in our complex modern society."[4] The National Interstate and Defense Highways Act of 1956, the largest public works program in U.S. history, became one of the principal achievements of his presidency. It stretched more than 3,000 miles from east to west and more than 1,900 miles north to south. On an annual basis, a quarter of the country's interstate auto traffic currently travels on the Eisenhower highway system.[5]

Civil rights were an even greater hurdle for him to deal with. By the 1950s, black impatience with racial segregation across the South was mounting and the Reverend Martin Luther King Jr., the head of the Southern Christian Leadership Conference (SCLC), was leading passive resistance to southern race laws. In May 1954, when the

the age of twelve would get along in an integrated school. The following year, 80 percent of white southerners remained opposed to integration in schools or in public transportation, and 55 percent said they could not imagine a time when they would see racial integration across their region. The South was awash in highway signs urging impeachment of Supreme Court chief justice Earl Warren, who was seen as the principal architect of the 1954 school desegregation decision. But a series of racial clashes across the South began to change public opinion. By 1957, a majority of the country approved of integrating the schools, but only "gradually." By the following summer, a plurality of the country thought the situation in the South would get worse. Still, a majority of Americans believed that sit-ins at lunch counters and "freedom riders" opposing segregated interstate travel were hurting black chances of achieving a prompt end to segregation.

Despite the national reluctance to press forward rapidly with racial integration, Eisenhower believed that the states had to defer to Washington's commands, above all court orders eliminating constitutional violations. The great test of his resolve to support federal authority over states' rights came in 1957 when Arkansas governor Orval Faubus resisted a court-ordered integration of Little Rock's Central High School, by directing Arkansas National Guardsmen to block nine black students from entering the school. Ike responded by announcing his constitutional duty to enforce the court's order: He federalized the Arkansas National Guard and directed them to facilitate rather than block the integration of the school. Faubus then removed the Arkansas Guardsmen from the school, but did nothing to restrain a white mob threatening violence against the black students. Because Ike did not think that the Arkansas troops would facilitate desegregation, he directed the 101st Airborne Division to fly to Little Rock to enforce the court's orders. Ike then went on television to tell the nation that the troops were there to prevent "demagogic extremists and disorderly mobs" from defying the law. In private he told aides that he was facing a choice between anarchy and the rule of law. But he would have been a more effective leader on civil rights, the most divisive national problem, had he been more outspoken about the need for public acceptance of equal racial treatment under the law.[6]

For Eisenhower, domestic issues, whether about the economy or race relations, paled alongside the Cold War. As a military chief who had firsthand knowledge of the cost in blood and treasure war extracted from every country, he was eager to find peaceful solutions to international problems. Immediately after being elected, he fulfilled his promise to go to Korea, flying over the front line dividing U.S. and South Korean forces from the entrenched Chinese and North Korean troops. It was clear to him that communist defenses would make an allied offensive a costly operation. The U.S. had already suffered more than seventy-five thousand casualties, which were certain to mount as long as the fighting continued. Eisenhower was also clear on the anti-war mood that gripped the United States, saying to one of his commanders in Korea, "I have a mandate from the people to stop the fighting." As important, he was eager to address other foreign policy questions, particularly how to avoid a nuclear conflict with the Soviet Union. Ike gave out "hints" that the Chinese would face atomic bombings if the Korean conflict continued. Stalin's death in March 1953 and expressions of interest from the Kremlin to reduce tensions in relations with the United States further heightened Chinese fears of defeat and dependence on the Soviet Union. Eventually, the Chinese would resume peace talks with Washington that produced an armistice in July. By then, more than thirty-three thousand U.S. troops had died, with another five thousand listed as missing in action.[7]

Although the Eisenhower campaign led by Nixon had denounced containment as cowardly, suggesting his administration would roll back communism or liberate the East European countries from Soviet control, Ike had no intention of provoking Moscow by overturning its sphere of control gained through its sacrifices in World War II. Like Truman, he was determined to contain them from expanding into Western Europe, the Middle East, and especially Latin America, which seemed most vulnerable to subversion. Convinced that the Korean War demonstrated American public impatience with limited wars, and determined not to face the possibility again of ending a small war with nuclear weapons, the Eisenhower administration took up the idea of "massive retaliation." In short, Soviet Russia and Communist China were put on notice that if provoked into a conflict, the United States intended to rely on its superiority in weapons of mass destruction.

What made an immediate difference in shaping Ike's foreign policy was Stalin's sudden death. His principal successor Georgy Malenkov announced the Kremlin's interest in "peaceful coexistence." Although it would take more than two years before both sides could give greater meaning to the phrase, they came together for a summit meeting in Geneva, Switzerland, in July 1955. Eisenhower had signaled his interest in reducing the arms race with Moscow by declaring, "Every gun that is made, every warship launched, every rocket fired signifies, in the final sense, a theft from those who hunger and are not fed, who are cold and not clothed."

By the time of the meeting, Nikita Khrushchev had become the Soviet leader and Ike urged him to accept "Open Skies," a plan giving both sides access to each other's airspace to track airfields and facilities that could launch nuclear weapons. Fearful of revealing how far behind they were to the United States in military capacity,

Khrushchev rejected the proposal as a "transparent espionage device." Eisenhower and Secretary of State John Foster Dulles had gone to Geneva determined not to be caught on camera smiling while with any of the Soviet leaders. They not only wanted to convince the Kremlin that they were as tough as them but also to shield themselves from charges at home that they had gone soft on communism. Although both sides wanted to tamp down the Cold War, neither was prepared to describe a new era of détente, and the mutual suspicions put a freeze on any major breakthrough in relations.[8]

Clandestine U.S. actions to topple unfriendly regimes in Iran and Guatemala further fanned Soviet suspicions of U.S. determination to defeat the Soviet Union. The Eisenhower government was as suspicious of Soviet intentions, believing it was set upon undermining pro-Western governments everywhere in order to bring them into the communist orbit. Consequently, the White House directed the Central Intelligence Agency to secretly work against pro-Soviet or anti-American governments in strategic regions around the globe, particularly in Iran, Guatemala, and Vietnam. Eisenhower saw these proxy conflicts as the best way to sustain the containment policy and avoid a major confrontation with Moscow.

Initially, the CIA targeted Mohammad Mossadegh's government in Tehran. Difficulties with Iran revolved around oil supplies, which amounted to 90 percent of Europe's petroleum products. It was a lucrative business that principally served British interests through the Anglo-Iranian Oil Company. Iran's shah, Reza Pahlavi, had made the deal with Britain in 1933, which did more to favor Iran's royal family than the country's national interest. By 1951, a movement led by Mossadegh to nationalize the oil company in Iran dominated the country's politics. The Truman administration urged London to negotiate a settlement with Mossadegh, but Churchill, who was back in power, refused, and when Eisenhower became president, the United States, in one of the greatest misjudgments in Ike's two terms, accepted London's assertion that the ouster of British control over Iran's oil represented a victory for the country's communists and a Soviet inroad into the Middle East. The White House responded with a CIA plot to topple Mossadegh. Fomenting street violence and funneling money to Shah Mohammad Reza Pahlavi, in August 1953, the CIA drove Mossadegh from power and arranged a succession government under the shah that negotiated a new oil contract with the West.[9]

Twenty-six years later, when a new surge of nationalism in Iran ousted the shah from power and established an anti-American Islamic government under the Ayatollah Khomeini, the U.S. and Iran fell into a six-decade period of estrangement that is still unresolved and intensified in January 2020 after the Trump administration assassinated Iran's military chief.

In the same vein, although it was meant to ensure the safety of the hemisphere from communist infiltration, Eisenhower's policy toward Guatemala poorly served U.S. relations with Latin America. In 1951, Jacobo Arbenz won a landslide election for the presidency of Guatemala. In the impoverished nation, where laborers earned twenty-six cents a day, the Arbenz government challenged the dominance of the United Fruit Company that controlled the country's principal banana crop. The government's expropriation of the company's uncultivated land moved United's president to say that it was now a contest between communism and "the right of property, the life and security of the Western Hemisphere." Eisenhower's State Department was all too ready to accept the challenge. Secretary of State John Foster Dulles and his brother Allen Dulles, the head of the CIA, had financial ties to United Fruit. The CIA went to work designing a countercoup against Arbenz, training and arming Guatemalan insurgents in Honduras and supplying aircraft for use in a coup in Nicaragua. In 1954, the successful takeover of the government by the wholly U.S.-armed, -financed, and -controlled insurgency was falsely characterized in the United States as an entirely Guatemalan affair. Guatemalans and most Latin Americans knew better. The coup is now a historical embarrassment to the Eisenhower administration and the United States. And it further radicalized Latin America, especially Cuba.[10]

At the same time Washington interfered in Iran and Guatemala, it took up the cause of defending South Vietnam from communist insurgents supplied by Ho Chi Minh's communist government in the North. The opposition to French colonial rule in Vietnam had reached a climax in 1954 at Dien Bien Phu. While Ike was opposed to putting U.S. troops in Indochina, he was eager to assure against French surrender, invoking the domino theory that if Vietnam fell to the communists, it would be the first of several countries to follow, meaning that all of Southeast Asia—Cambodia, Laos, Burma, Thailand, Malaya, and Indonesia—would be threatened with collapse. The White House solution was a coalition of Western states arranging a settlement that promised independence for Vietnam or an end to colonial rule. But that proved out of reach, as was the French request to the United States to unleash its air power against the insurgents, including a possible use of atomic bombs. "We can't use those awful things against Asians for the second time in less than ten years," Ike said. He was also determined to shield the United States from being labeled a proponent of colonial rule. America's refusal to bomb the Viet Minh (the North Vietnamese communists) sealed the fate of the French, who surrendered in May 1954 and agreed to divide the Vietnamese peninsula at the seventeenth parallel into North and South Vietnam.[11]

In the aftermath of the settlement that divided the peninsula, the Eisenhower administration devoted itself to preserving South Vietnam from a communist insurgency that threatened the beginnings of Ike's domino prediction. It was not just the president who voiced a concern about Vietnam's independence, it was the accepted wisdom of the time across party lines, including Massachusetts Democratic senator John F. Kennedy, who publicly called South Vietnam the "finger in the dike" against the "Red Tide" in Asia. In 1954, the Eisenhower administration negotiated the creation of the Southeast Asia Treaty Organization (SEATO), an obvious counterpart to NATO, to stand against further communist expansion in Asia. The administration now also threw its support behind Ngo Dinh Diem, the Catholic president of South Vietnam's Buddhist majority. It poured in money and military equipment worth over a billion dollars to help build a stable anti-communist nation—a task many saw as a fool's errand. But it shored up an unstable country for the time being. How long it would last, however, was a matter for future administrations to confront.[12]

At home, Eisenhower had to deal with McCarthyism—the anticommunist crusade that besmirched innocent people. Never interested in facts that refuted his charges, McCarthy recklessly threw out accusations that resonated with millions of Americans agitated by Cold War fears. Eisenhower, who refused "to get into the gutter with that guy," adopted a public policy of silence about McCarthy's tactics. Ike believed that "only a short-sighted or completely inexperienced individual would urge the use of the office of the Presidency to give an opponent the publicity he so avidly desires. . . . I have no intention whatsoever of helping promote the publicity value of anyone who disagrees with me—demagogue or not!" C. D. Jackson, a principal presidential aide, called Ike's attitude toward McCarthy the "Three Little Monkeys act: poor tactics, poor strategy, and poor arithmetic." As some historians believe, Ike's tactic of ignoring McCarthy helped undermine and ruin McCarthy in the 1954 Army-McCarthy congressional hearings. At the same time, however, historian Blanche Wiesen Cook maintains that McCarthyism was advanced and intensified by Eisenhower's determination to ignore it, and by McCarthy's reckless attacks on alleged American supporters of communism.[13] Whether McCarthy would have been undermined more quickly by Eisenhower's open opposition to him is difficult to say. But given Eisenhower's popularity and image as a sensible leader, it seems likely that criticism of McCarthy's abusive language in overdrawn attacks would have turned a majority of Americans against him before the Army-McCarthy hearings brought him down.

Along with McCarthy's agitation about the communist danger, which excited talk of a possible war to destroy Soviet Russia, came international crises that provoked further talk of military action against Moscow. In October 1956, after Nikita Khrushchev acknowledged the crimes of Josef Stalin's rule and Polish patriots responded to U.S. propaganda encouraging liberation from Soviet domination by turning out a pro-Soviet government, a rebellion erupted in communist-controlled Hungary. When Moscow sent troops and tanks to Budapest to maintain its control in Hungary and signal its determination to hold on to its sphere of influence across Eastern Europe, the U.S. considered providing arms to the beleaguered Hungarians. But Ike vetoed the proposal as risking a wider war with the Soviet Union. It was one thing to contain communism by surreptitious means in Iran, Guatemala, and Vietnam. It was another thing entirely to attempt to roll back or liberate areas of Soviet dominance gained by the victory in World War II, directly threatening their national security or what historical experience told them was essential to Soviet safety. The setback to Soviet international standing amid predictions that Soviet communism would eventually succumb to its own failings moved Khrushchev to declare publicly that Moscow would "outlast" capitalism or, as Khrushchev was quoted across the West, "We will bury you."

A conflict at the same time between Egypt, which had nationalized the Suez Canal passageway between the Middle East and Asia, and Britain, France, and Israel, posed another problem. If the United States were to give tacit approval by allowing Egyptian defeat and return of the canal to Western control, it would enflame the Arab world and jeopardize Middle East oil supplies. It would also give Moscow an opening wedge to expand its influence in the region at the expense of the democracies. It was another form of containment to keep Moscow from increasing its influence in the oil-rich Arab Middle East. Ike thought that "France and Britain have made a terrible mistake." The Suez crisis escalated into a wider dilemma when Moscow threatened to send forces to the Middle East to restore peace if the aggressors did not agree to a cease-fire. The White House responded with a warning to the Russians to stay out of the conflict and asserted that only an international force under the banner of the United Nations should police the region. By using financial means to undermine the British pound, the White House forced London into a cease-fire followed by French and Israeli compliance. When the British seemed to be dragging their feet about taking their troops out of Egypt, Ike successfully threatened Prime Minister Anthony Eden with further crippling of the international value of the pound.[14]

Although Ike had headed off greater Soviet penetration of the Middle East, he struggled to continue containing Soviet expansion in Europe and maintain an advantage over them in missile technology. In October 1957, Moscow raised its international profile as a modern nation with unmatched military capacity by putting a satellite in space—Sputnik. Although the successful orbit of the Earth by a 184-pound device was an amazing advance in potential space exploration, it did not readily translate into advanced technology in intercontinental ballistic missiles (ICBMs). To be sure, the Soviets were moving in that direction, but they were far behind the United States in capacity to deliver nuclear weapons to any point on the globe. Nevertheless, the Soviet achievement in space sent a chill of concern through the West. It echoed in the famous "kitchen debate" in July 1959 that Vice President Richard Nixon had with Nikita Khrushchev at a U.S. exhibit in Moscow on consumer products, or more to the point on whether the American capitalist or the Soviet communist system was superior in serving the creature comforts of average citizens.

The central controversy in Europe was over Berlin. The city had been partitioned into four zones since the end of the war, with Soviet control in East Germany and East Berlin. For Moscow, the arrangement had become a source of embarrassment and growing concern. The better-educated population of the East European satellite countries, but especially of East Germany, were migrating in droves through East Berlin to the West, where they saw a chance for a better life. With no limits on movement within the city of Berlin, the East German population had shrunk by three million in the years after 1945. The Soviets responded by calling for the evacuation of all allied forces from Berlin, which was 110 miles inside the East German zone, and its reunification under East German control. Khrushchev began setting deadlines for when all occupation forces should depart. But these came and went without incident.[15]

Still Berlin threatened to turn into a showdown at some time in the future. Because keeping the peace remained Eisenhower's and Khrushchev's highest priority, they agreed to exchange visits and engage in talks that might reduce their differences or at least show that each had a human face. In 1959, they agreed to a ten-day visit to the United States by Khrushchev, whose capacity for theatrics was the equal of any leader on the international scene. Three days before he arrived in Washington, the Soviets successfully fired a rocket that reached the moon. To underscore their superiority in rocketry, Khrushchev gave Ike a gift of a miniature replica of the spacecraft.

Because a foreign ministers meeting in Geneva had made no progress on Berlin or any other issue dividing East and West, Ike was initially reluctant to have Khrushchev become the first Soviet head of state to travel to the United States. But willing to go "an extra mile" for peace, he agreed to the visit. An outcry across America and Europe about letting the devil in the front door persuaded Ike to visit London, Paris, and Bonn (West Germany's capital) before Khrushchev arrived in Washington, partly to remind Europeans that the U.S. was aligned with them against Soviet Russia and partly to blunt Khrushchev's public diplomacy. Ike's capacity for stirring public sympathy, especially in countries that recalled his contribution to defeating Nazi Germany, was more than a match for Khrushchev's popular appeal.

Khrushchev visited seven cities in the United States and enjoyed the daily newspaper and television coverage, which boosted his international standing. Cartoonist Herblock caught the American response to the visit with a cartoon of Ike and Khrushchev riding in an open car waving to crowds each with his fingers crossed. But Ike was not content with a public Khrushchev tour that left all their differences unsettled, and insisted on three days of talks at Camp David, the presidential retreat in Maryland's Catoctin Mountain. The discussions yielded a Khrushchev concession to give up any ultimatum on Berlin in the expectation that they would solve the German problem together, and they discussed the need for an arms control agreement to rein in their mutually expensive military budgets. They also agreed to follow up with a Paris summit in May 1960 that would include Britain and France. The domestic results of the visit were a great success. Where 50 percent of a survey approved of Khrushchev coming to the United States, by the close of the visit 64 percent endorsed the meeting and Eisenhower's approval went up from 57 to 66 percent, while 58 percent said that if Ike could run again for a third term, they would vote for him.[16]

Camp David was the last congenial summit meeting of the Eisenhower presidency, and a reciprocal visit to the Soviet Union by Eisenhower never occurred. In May 1960, a U-2 American spy plane flying over the Soviet Union was shot down by a new Soviet surface-to-air missile. Francis Gary Powers, the pilot, was captured and imprisoned. The Eisenhower administration initially lied about the plane's purposes, saying it was only a weather reconnaissance aircraft that had strayed 1,200 miles into the Soviet Union. But Moscow revealed that it had the pilot, a CIA operative, in custody, and the plane's films showing Soviet air bases. Ike now had to acknowledge that America had been spying on the Soviets for several years, not because of any offensive design but out of a need to defend itself against a possible Soviet attack.

Moscow, which felt perpetually threatened by a more powerful United States, dismissed Ike's explanation as untrue and launched a propaganda campaign against U.S. "aggression." At the Paris meeting later in May, Khrushchev engaged in a forty-five-minute harangue against Ike, saying, "How can I invite as a dear guest the leader of a country which has committed an aggressive act against us?" When Eisenhower reiterated his explanation that the United States was only intent on defending itself against a Soviet surprise attack and promised to end U-2 overflights of Russia, which had been made obsolete anyway by new spy satellites, Khrushchev and his delegation walked out of the room. They assumed correctly that the United States had developed a fresh means to oversee Soviet military installations. For all practical purposes, the conference was at an end, or, more to the point, the Khrushchev-Eisenhower diplomatic exchanges were over. Khrushchev said that he would wait for the next administration to resume discussions with the United States.[17]

In the meantime, the Eisenhower administration had a new problem to deal with closer to home—the rise of a revolutionary regime in Havana, Cuba, under the leadership of a charismatic anti-American leader, Fidel Castro. In 1957, in an interview with a *New York Times* reporter, Castro described himself as nationalistic, anti-imperialist, and anti-colonial. So, in January 1959, when Castro ousted Cuba's long-time dictator Fulgencio Batista from power, Ike's advisers debated whether Castro was a communist and a Soviet tool penetrating America's sphere of control or just another anti-American leftist. A Castro visit to the United States in April 1959 did little to answer the question. But Richard Nixon, who had seen anti-American demonstrations during a visit to Central America in 1958, believed that Castro was a closet communist and recommended overthrowing him. Shortly after, at the same time that Eisenhower recognized the new government and pledged to promote good relations with it, he ordered the training and arming of Cuban exiles in Guatemala in preparation for an invasion of the island to overturn Castro's rule. By 1960, it was clear that Castro had allied himself with Moscow, and in September 1960, in the first-ever televised debate between presidential candidates, John F. Kennedy, the Democrat, pilloried Nixon and the Eisenhower administration for failing to take a harder line with Castro. Soon after, when Eisenhower briefed President-Elect Kennedy on Cuba, he said, "We cannot let the present government there go on."[18]

Ike had similar advice on Laos, the small landlocked country in Southeast Asia where a civil war between competing factions, including communists, made the country a part of the Cold War rivalry. The Eisenhower administration had been wrestling with challenges about Southeast Asia and Cambodia, Laos, and Vietnam in particular since the early fifties. Eisenhower opposed using atom bombs to defeat communist insurgents in the region or sending in American ground forces to fight what looked like an endless struggle against indigenous forces. When Ike met with Kennedy in January 1961, he told him, "Any time you permit Communists to have a part in the government of such a nation, they end up in control." Ike also described Laos as "the cork in the bottle. If Laos fell, then Thailand, the Philippines," and even Chiang Kai-shek's Formosa would be vulnerable. Eisenhower had no answer to the question, "What to do?" to prevent a communist advance in Southeast Asia beyond backing an independent South Vietnam and helping anyone opposed to the communists in Cambodia and Laos.

Although Eisenhower left Kennedy knotty problems in Cuba and Southeast Asia as well as a stumbling American economy in recession and 50 percent of Americans saying there was still "much danger" of a war, he finished his term with 50 percent thinking it was possible for the United States to work out its differences with the

Soviet Union, 59 percent approving of his presidential performance, and 65 percent of the country believing he was either a "great" or at minimum a "good" president. Only 7 percent considered him a "poor" president.

In the subsequent six decades, set alongside Presidents Kennedy, Johnson, Nixon, Ford, Carter, Reagan, the two Bushes, Clinton, Obama, and Trump, Eisenhower continues to command regard as a wise president who served the nation better than most chief executives. True, he was too cautious about addressing issues of segregation and racial equality, though his passivity cannot be seen as an inducement to any future president to ignore civil rights. But unlike some presidents, Ike never left people puzzled about what he hoped to achieve in foreign affairs; there was never any question about Eisenhower's determination to protect America's national interest.

Every aspirant for the White House does well to learn how earlier presidents advanced the national well-being; but slogans are never enough to convince people of a president's determination to meet foreign threats. We can only imagine how unhappy Ike would have been about a president who shows little regard for NATO and the alliance system that has served America's interests for seventy years, or shows himself ready to appease a foreign power at odds with U.S. interests. Ike would also have recommended knowing Mark Twain's observation that history doesn't repeat itself but it does rhyme, meaning that a president should know about past events and be prepared to sustain them in the national interest.[19]

While Eisenhower enjoys a positive historical reputation as president, especially alongside several of the presidents who followed, his presidency was not without shortcomings. Most regrettable were his secret interference in Iran and his proxy war in Vietnam. The Iran policy made Iran a perpetual enemy and difficult adversary in the

Middle East, whereas as recently as 2020 the United States and Iran came to the edge of an all-out war. Vietnam was worse, drawing us into a ten-year jungle war that cost the United Sates more than fifty thousand lives and an embarrassing military defeat. These failings cannot be overlooked in assessing Eisenhower's presidency.

CHAPTER 6

John F. Kennedy

The Making of an Icon

———

In the 1960 presidential campaign, the forty-three-year-old Massachusetts senator John F. Kennedy, the Democratic nominee, battled Republican complaints that he was too young; too inexperienced; and a Catholic whose patriotism was suspect, because allegedly a Catholic's first loyalty was to the pope in Rome. Even at the time, the complaints seemed overdrawn. After all, Theodore Roosevelt was a few months younger than Kennedy when he succeeded William McKinley, and TR had become the most admired president since Lincoln. Moreover, Kennedy's six years in the House and eight in the Senate outran TR's experience or that of William Howard Taft, Calvin Coolidge, or Herbert Hoover in elected office. As for patriotism, as Kennedy himself said, nobody asked his brother his religion when he lost his life on a dangerous mission over England in World War II; nor did they acknowledge Kennedy's own navy combat service in the Pacific that won him commendations. Although he was a compulsive womanizer, it was not a topic that mainstream news organizations discussed in the 1960s; nor did it have any significant impact on his candidacy or his presidency. An extramarital affair with a twenty-two-year-old White House intern did not surface until forty years after his presidency.

John Kennedy learned politics by first running for the House of Representatives in 1946. He was not keen to enter the give and take of an election campaign or the harsh competition of a Democratic Party primary in Boston. It was not that he shied away from political rivalry; like his father, Joe, he enjoyed taking on opponents or besting them. But he was more interested in the world of ideas and book writing. If his older brother Joe, Jr., hadn't died in the war, he would have been the family politician and Jack probably would have been a journalist or author. He had published his Harvard senior honor's thesis, "Why England Slept," which had become a bestseller despite suspicions that it was ghostwritten, and after the war, he had covered the founding of the United Nations in 1945 for several newspapers. As a result of travel abroad and time spent in England when his father was the U.S. ambassador in London, he was much more interested in foreign affairs than domestic problems. He once told Richard Nixon that an increase in the minimum wage was of little interest to him compared to issues of war and peace, saying, "Who gives a shit if the minimum wage is $1.15 or $1.25?" When he first served in Congress, where he said little about overseas issues, he complained, "We were just worms in the House—nobody paid much attention to us nationally."

During six years in the lower chamber, he was already focused on a U.S. Senate seat. But once in the Senate, after a hard-fought campaign in 1952 against sitting Massachusetts Republican senator Henry Cabot Lodge, he was still discontented. He thought being a senator was "the most corrupting job in the world," seeing the men—almost all men—as all too ready to favor the interests that financed their expensive campaigns. Nor did he think most of them were world-beaters when it came to intelligence. He enjoyed quoting Senate chaplain Edward Everett Hale: When asked if he prayed for the senators, Hale replied, "No, I look at the senators and I pray for the country." Kennedy, with the luxury of a rich father who could finance his campaigns, could remain independent of any special interest, except for those in his state that could align against his re-election.

Besides, Kennedy kept his focus on foreign affairs and the Cold War with the Soviet Union. It impressed him as the best path to the presidency, which was his ultimate goal. But to get there, he needed to reach accommodation with the liberal wing of his party, which, under the spell of Adlai Stevenson, focused on defending liberals from the attacks of Joseph McCarthy and on the civil rights fight to advance equality for African Americans. To create distance from his father, who was identified as a wealthy, conservative, anti-communist Democrat, and anti-Semite, and win backing from party liberals, Kennedy hired Ted Sorensen, a brilliant Nebraska progressive lawyer, as an aide and speechwriter.

At the same time, Kennedy fixed his attention on foreign challenges. In 1954, the second year of his Senate tenure, a majority of Americans were primarily concerned about the threat of war, communist subversion, and national defense: the issues Eisenhower seemed best able to address. Kennedy favored higher defense spending as a deterrent to war, and opposition to colonialism that was gripping Third World countries in Africa, Asia, and Latin America. He agreed with liberal Democrats that the United States could not preserve its standing as the conscience of the world if it identified itself in any way with Western imperialism, which had become anathema to developing countries. Like a majority of Americans, he believed that the Cold War was in significant part a contest for "hearts and minds" in former and existing colonies. Kennedy found confirmation for his view in the failing French fight to preserve power in Indochina. He opposed any U.S. military involvement in the region and made himself a leading Senate spokesman for self-determination in Cambodia, Laos, and Vietnam.

While his credentials as a war hero and his outspoken foreign policy views gave him standing as a potential presidential candidate, his caution in 1954 on Senate condemnation of Joe McCarthy aroused complaints that he was a faux liberal. Eleanor Roosevelt, making reference to Kennedy's 1956 Pulitzer Prize–winning book, *Profiles in Courage*, about senators who had risked their political careers by defending unpopular causes, said that Kennedy would do well to show less profile and more courage. Nonetheless, he was able to battle his way to the nomination, particularly by winning the West Virginia primary, a state with a 97 percent Protestant population, demonstrating to Democratic Party bosses that a Catholic could win a national election.

Nothing may have been more instrumental in advancing his 1960 presidential campaign against Richard Nixon, however, than the first televised presidential debate in September. Understanding that it was less the command of debate topics than the image of someone who seemed more presidential that would make a difference, Kennedy's team made sure that his confident and attractive appearance contrasted sharply with Nixon's, who, someone said, looked like they had embalmed him before he died. And it gave Kennedy an edge in a close race. Kennedy won the White House by only 118,000 popular votes out of sixty-eight million ballots with 303 electoral votes from twenty-two states, to Nixon's 219 from twenty-eight states.

The narrow victory persuaded Kennedy to appoint Republicans

to high administration positions: Robert McNamara, the president of the Ford Motor Company, as secretary of defense; and McGeorge Bundy, Harvard's dean of faculty, as national security adviser. Despite his small margin of votes over Nixon, Kennedy quickly enjoyed majority support in opinion polls and worked to expand that advantage in the first months of his presidency. Kennedy increased his appeal with idealistic proposals—a Peace Corps and an Alliance for Progress in Latin America—that resonated with the country's better angels.

But Kennedy put his popularity in jeopardy when he agreed to follow through on an Eisenhower plan to topple Fidel Castro in Cuba by unleashing Cuban exiles trained and armed by the CIA. Despite assurances from his intelligence agencies that an invasion at Cuba's Bay of Pigs, on the island's southern coast, would touch off a rebellion overturning Castro, it was a miscalculation: Over a hundred invaders were killed and another 1,300 were captured and imprisoned. When Kennedy openly took responsibility for the failure, his approval rating jumped to 83 percent. He joked, "The worse I do, the more popular I get."

Yet whatever his standing, he did not back away from bold ideas. In May 1961, he proposed to land a man on the moon and return him to Earth by the end of the decade. It was aimed not only at restoring America's international prestige as a world leader in technology, but also as a way to boost the economy with advances in weather forecasting and electronic communications. It would provide jobs in the South and the West, where much of the work would be done and the economy needed stimulating. The proposal triggered complaints about the billions that could be spent to improve conditions in America and around the world. But Kennedy took the longer view: When he labeled his administration the New Frontier, he intended to follow innovative paths that marked his presidency as continuing the country's tradition of reaching beyond what had come before.

Kennedy also hoped to bypass the stale clichés that informed Cold War thinking by traveling to Europe to meet first with France's President Charles de Gaulle and then Russia's Nikita Khrushchev. For the young Kennedy, de Gaulle was something of an icon. His leadership of the Free French during the time of defeat in World War II, and his restoration of France as a major power after the war, had established him, in Kennedy's words, as "a great captain of the Western World." Mindful that de Gaulle did not trust America's commitment to defend Western Europe against Soviet Russia, Kennedy wished to assure him that the United States was determined to contain Moscow's expansionist intentions. He also hoped to promote his own public standing as a skilled leader with images of him conferring with the French president. Understanding perfectly what Kennedy wanted from the visit after his setback in Cuba, de Gaulle turned the visit into a public pageant, and at a formal dinner he praised Kennedy's "energy and drive" and "intelligence and courage." In private, he told Kennedy to consult advisers but to rely on himself for policy decisions. He also warned the young president against involvement in Southeast Asia as a potential "military and political quagmire."

A month into his administration, when Kennedy sat down with Soviet experts in preparation for a conference, he displayed "a mentality extraordinarily free of preconceived prejudices." He thought "there must be some basis upon which [the United States and Soviet Union] . . . could live without blowing each other up." To that end, he had agreed to meet with Soviet leader Nikita Khrushchev in Vienna in June 1961.

As Kennedy learned, having expert advice doesn't insulate a president from blunders. But it gave Kennedy a basis for curbing the negative results of the Vienna talks. Kennedy was urged not to debate Khrushchev about their competing ideologies, but as someone who never dodged a challenge, Kennedy argued the virtues of capitalism versus communism. It was not so much that Khrushchev had the better arguments as that he had a particular talent for bullying opponents. After the first session, when one of Kennedy's aides said, "You seemed pretty calm while he was giving you a hard time," an exasperated Kennedy responded, "What did you expect me to do? Take off one of my shoes and hit him over the head with it?" It was a reference to Khrushchev's performance at the United Nations in October 1960 when he banged a shoe on a desk to underscore a point. At the end of the first day of talks, Kennedy privately complained to his Moscow ambassador, "He treated me like a little boy, like a little boy. Is it always like this?" he asked. The remaining days of the conference were hardly a lovefest, but Kennedy held his ground when Khrushchev tried to bait him into another debate about their respective systems. "Look, Mr. Chairman," Kennedy said, "you aren't going to make a communist out of me and I don't expect to make a capitalist out of you, so let's get down to business."

The business was principally about arms control, or a test ban on nuclear weapons that were polluting the atmosphere and spurring an arms race. They were also at odds over Berlin, 110 miles inside the East German communist zone. More embarrassed than ever about educated residents in the East fleeing to the West through Berlin, Khrushchev wanted to sign a treaty that unified Berlin and brought it under the full control of the East German Democratic Republic, the GDR, a Soviet satellite. It was out of the question for the West to cede West Berlin to communist control or allow the Soviets to close off access to West Berlin through the 110-mile East German corridor, which Khrushchev threatened if no treaty was signed. Kennedy pressed him not to upset the existing balance in Europe. But Khrushchev was unrelenting and warned Kennedy against provoking a war. Neither could agree who might be bringing the world to the brink of war, and when Khrushchev ended by saying that it was up to the U.S. to decide whether there would be war, Kennedy replied, "Then Mr. Chairman, there will be war. It will be a cold winter."

Kennedy did not find much solace at home. His proposals to Congress for a tax cut that would reduce the top rate from 91 to 71 percent found little appeal in a Congress eager to reduce the national debt. Nor did his request for a seniors' health insurance measure find support. Although Democrats controlled both houses of Congress, warnings against socialized medicine that raised fears of state control made "Medicare" a reach too far. Nothing, however, agitated the conservative southern Democratic committee chairmen more than a proposal for federal aid to education, which they feared could turn into an assault on segregation beyond *Brown v. Board of Education*, leaving this proposal short of congressional approval.

As for civil rights, which had become increasingly controversial as Martin Luther King's SCLC pressed its nonviolent campaign for equal treatment in all places of public accommodation, the topic had become too toxic for Kennedy to challenge southern Democrats in Congress. He also hoped that if he held off putting a civil rights bill before Congress, it would make southern Democrats less resistant to his proposals for Medicare and aid to education. He was wrong. Besides, a continuing campaign of violence against black and white civil rights activists across the South added to the sense of crisis about race relations in America. In September 1962, a confrontation in Oxford, Mississippi, over attempts to enroll James Meredith, a black air force veteran, in the University of Mississippi, resulted in riots that cost two lives. Although Kennedy's insistence on enforcing federal court orders won a temporary victory, it was hardly the end of racial conflict across the region that tested Kennedy's leadership.

A small number of people close to Kennedy who knew that he suffered from a variety of lifelong health problems worried that the burdens of the public crises besetting his administration might overwhelm him. Since childhood, he had been afflicted by chronic spastic colitis. When Kennedy was twenty, steroids helped control his colitis, but it triggered Addison's disease, the malfunctioning of the adrenal gland, and the onset of osteoporosis of the lumbar spine, which produced constant back pain. Between 1955 and 1957, he was hospitalized nine times for forty-four days, including one nineteen-day stay and twice for a week. Addison's, back miseries, colitis, prostatitis, and urinary tract infections made his health a constant problem.

None of this had been enough to deter him from running for president in 1960, though it was largely hidden from the public and most everyone else. When Senator Ted Kennedy read my 2003 biography of his brother, he told me that he didn't know the extent of his brother's illnesses. During his presidential campaign, when a medical bag containing Kennedy's numerous medications was misplaced, he was frantic to recover it lest it fall into the wrong hands and reveal the extent of his health woes. Forty years after Kennedy's passing, keeping the full story of Kennedy's health issues a secret remained a priority that could not withstand the opening of his health records in his presidential library. Kennedy thus joined a long tradition of presidents before and since—Cleveland, Wilson, FDR, LBJ, and perhaps Reagan—who hid their health difficulties.

Nothing during Kennedy's term of office tested his health more than a missile crisis with Russia over Cuba. In the spring and early summer of 1962, the Soviets convinced Castro to let them deploy forty medium- and intermediate-range nuclear missiles on the island.

Purportedly to protect Castro's Cuba from a U.S. invasion to topple his government, it was meant primarily to balance America's advantage in ICBMs. Kennedy understood that the Soviet missiles represented an intrusion into America's sphere of control that changed the military balance of power, or at least the perception of that balance. After a U-2 spy plane detected the construction sites and New York Republican senator Kenneth Keating publicly criticized the administration for doing nothing in response, Kennedy warned that if these were offensive weapons, "the gravest issues would arise." Determined to avoid a nuclear war with Russia, Kennedy resisted demands for a prompt invasion of Cuba or a blockade, which would have been an act of war. Repeated Soviet assurances that they were emplacing only defensive weapons on the island did not deter Kennedy from authorizing additional U-2 flights over Cuba.

On October 16, it became clear to the Kennedy White House that the Soviets were building offensive missile sites in Cuba. Kennedy now faced a showdown with Khrushchev that could either eliminate the missile threat or lead to an attack on Cuba that could threaten a nuclear conflict. Kennedy, above all, was determined to remove the missiles from Cuba—preferably by negotiation, if necessary by a military strike. Secretary of Defense Robert McNamara urged a middle ground between military action and negotiation—a "declaration of open surveillance; a statement that we would immediately impose a blockade against offensive weapons entering Cuba in the future," though it would be called a "quarantine" rather than a blockade. Part of Kennedy's concern was that a blockade of Cuba could trigger a Soviet move against West Berlin. But the construction of a wall in 1961 that stemmed the tide of migration to the West had eased Moscow's Berlin problem. Adlai Stevenson, who was serving as Kennedy's ambassador to the United Nations, also cautioned against hasty action that could precipitate a crisis with Moscow.

Kennedy now stubbornly resisted pressure from his military chiefs to attack Cuba with air raids followed by an invasion. He wished to avoid military action, if possible, and his memories of the stumbling performance, in the Pacific, of the navy brass before the Midway victory in 1942, and poor advice from the military chiefs and CIA before the Bay of Pigs invasion, added to his reluctance to follow their suggestions. He was especially put off by air force chief Curtis LeMay, who opposed Kennedy's quarantine idea by saying, "This is almost as bad as the appeasement at Munich." He also declared his conviction that the Soviets would do nothing in response to an attack on Cuba. Afterward, Kennedy said to an aide, "Can you imagine LeMay saying a thing like that? These brass hats have one great advantage in their favor. If we listen to them . . . none of us will be alive later to tell them they were wrong."

Taking his own counsel, Kennedy announced that he would quarantine Cuba to prevent further shipments of offensive weapons into the country, and sent Khrushchev a letter insisting that he remove the missile bases and other offensive weapons already on the island. He added that he "assumed that you or any other sane man would [not], in this nuclear age, plunge the world into war which it is crystal clear no country could win and which could only result in catastrophic consequences to the whole world." At the same time, Kennedy addressed Americans on television, condemning the Soviets for lying and warning of retaliatory action if the Soviets used the missiles already in Cuba. Khrushchev's initial response was not encouraging, blaming the United States for the crisis. Kennedy responded by reaffirming his earlier warnings and proceeding with the quarantine.

The crisis eased when news arrived that Soviet ships carrying weapons to Cuba had turned around and retreated from a confrontation with American destroyers. With the White House secretly promising to remove U.S. medium-range nuclear missiles from Turkey in return for Soviet removal of its missile sites in Cuba, Khrushchev now declared himself prepared to withdraw the weapons if Washington pledged not to invade Cuba. The exchange ended the crisis, but not before Kennedy instructed his advisers not to gloat lest it embarrass the Soviets into other offensive actions to save face. Kennedy's response to the crisis was an act of statesmanship that spared the world from a horror too great to contemplate.

Kennedy hoped that his October success in the Cuban crisis would translate into Democratic victories in the November congressional elections and greater legislative receptivity to his domestic reforms on taxes, education, and health insurance for seniors. Indeed, his party did well in the midterm contests, gaining four Senate seats and losing only four House seats, which made this the best midterm result for any twentieth-century president other than FDR in 1934. Still, it guaranteed nothing, especially on civil rights, which was the most pressing domestic issue and still under the control of southern segregationists in the House and Senate. Despite the hundredth anniversary of the Emancipation Proclamation, blacks continued to suffer the economic and social limits of segregation. While Kennedy repeatedly urged action to protect voting rights and took executive action to advance equal treatment under the law, he continued to hope that rejecting pleas to put a civil rights bill before Congress would facilitate passage of his other legislative initiatives. It was a false hope.

Martin Luther King viewed the Kennedy administration as cautious and timid about defending civil rights. He said that counsels of wait or patience were tantamount to "never." His organization, the

SCLC, prodded the administration by launching an anti-segregation campaign in Birmingham, Alabama, one of the most racist communities in the South. Eugene "Bull" Connor, the city's police commissioner, spoiled for a fight with these "radicals," some of whom FBI director J. Edgar Hoover described as the advanced wave of communism. When Connor unleashed attack dogs against marchers, and firemen turned high-pressure hoses on them that tore off their clothes, the resulting images on television of the clash embarrassed the country before the world. Black rioting in response to the city's repression made the injustices of segregation a national and international issue. George Wallace, Alabama's die-hard segregationist governor, who had promised "segregation now, segregation tomorrow, segregation forever," sent in the Alabama National Guard, which defended the status quo.

Attorney General Robert Kennedy, the president's brother, warned that thirty southern cities could dissolve in violence in the summer of 1963 if the administration didn't act to head off black rioting with promises of remedial measures. On a visit to Alabama to mark the thirtieth anniversary of the TVA, President Kennedy conferred privately with Wallace, who refused to give any ground on segregation. Kennedy made it clear to photographers that he didn't want any photos of him with the governor. More substantively, Kennedy decided to ask Congress for a civil rights law that once and for all ended segregation in all places of public accommodation—public transportation, hotels, restaurants, movie theaters, swimming pools, lunch counters, etc. When advisers had urged him instead to make a public plea for white southern officeholders and businessmen to meet with black leaders about jobs and integration, Kennedy said it was "hopeless, they'll never reform." It was time for the federal government to take a definitive stand. In June, when a crisis erupted over integrating the

University of Alabama, the last segregated state university in America, Kennedy went before the country in a televised address to make the case for his civil rights law.

Kennedy understood ever since he had bested Nixon in their September 1960 debate that TV was his ally. In 1961, he had begun holding live televised press conferences. Although some advisers warned him against the perils of televised interviews that could risk embarrassments that would hurt his standing, he knew that personal appearances on television were his political gold. Arthur Schlesinger, Jr. said the press conferences were "a superb show, always gay, often exciting, relished by the reporters and by the television audience."

On June 11, Kennedy gave a nationally televised Oval Office speech on behalf of a civil rights bill. Although he had little expectation that he could overcome southern congressional opposition with his rhetoric, he felt compelled to address the nation. "We are confronted primarily with a moral issue," he said. "It is as old as the scriptures and is as clear as the American Constitution. The heart of the question is whether all Americans are to be afforded equal rights and equal opportunities. . . . One hundred years of delay have passed since President Lincoln freed the slaves, yet their heirs, their grandsons, are not fully free. . . . And this Nation, for all its hopes and all its boasts, will not be fully free until all its citizens are free." He saw a great change "at hand, and our task, our obligation, is to make that revolution, that change, peaceful and constructive for all." On June 19, he put his bill before Congress. As anticipated, the southerners not only held it hostage but also bottled up other Kennedy reform proposals. He and brother Bobby thought it might cost him reelection. And yet they took solace from the thought that they had done the right thing, and that history would accord them plaudits for challenging the nation to give meaning to its better traditions.

Martin Luther King praised Kennedy's speech and followed up by organizing an August march on Washington. Kennedy worried that such a gathering would provoke violence and sidetrack his civil rights bill. But the march was peaceful and King delivered his brilliant "I Have a Dream" speech in the shadow of the Lincoln Memorial, concluding with the words of the old spiritual, "Free at last! Free at last! Thank God Almighty, we are free at last!" The speech and the large crowd's decorum won Kennedy's and the nation's admiration. Despite a bombing at a Birmingham church in September that killed four young black girls, it did little to change the congressional outlook. Kennedy's willingness to make compromises on the bill's provisions still left it in limbo for the rest of the year. He was so discouraged by the impasse that he told his secretary that, as she recalled, "he felt like packing his bags and leaving."

While civil rights opposition frustrated him, he had the satisfaction of seeing new gains in foreign affairs. He was determined to follow the resolution of the missile crisis with an improvement in Soviet-American relations. In June 1963, he used a commencement address at American University in Washington, D.C., to further reduce Cold War perils. It is now recalled as a great state paper about what he called the most important topic on earth, "world peace." He said it must not be a peace "enforced on the world by American weapons of war." Nor was he talking about "the peace of the grave or the security of the slave." In short, it was not to be peace imposed on adversaries by the threat or use of nuclear weapons; nor would it be the peace that came with appeasement of aggressors. Moreover, he hoped for not a temporary peace "but peace for all time." It would require not simply a more enlightened attitude by Moscow but a more accepting attitude by the United States. A Soviet-American war would do nothing but destroy "all we have built [and] all we have worked for," he said.

Although congressional Republicans dismissed the speech as "a soft line" and "a dreadful mistake," the Soviets hailed it as statesmanlike, and Khrushchev said it was "the best statement made by any president since Roosevelt." In the atmosphere of the Cold War, in which each side pilloried the other as consummate evil and ready to destroy the other, Kennedy's speech was a bold departure from the rhetoric of hate coming out of China, Russia, and the United States.

In the reach for better relations with Moscow, nothing seemed more important to Kennedy than persuading the Soviets to agree to a mutual test ban treaty on nuclear explosions that were poisoning the environment and fueling the arms race. In the summer of 1961, Moscow had announced a resumption of nuclear testing that had been on hold since 1958 after radioactive material had been found in food products. Although Kennedy told Americans that mankind had taken "into his mortal hands the power of self-extinction," the need for a sufficient deterrent persuaded him to announce the resumption of American testing too, especially after Moscow exploded a fifty-megaton bomb in November 1961 and carried out fifty atmospheric tests in sixty days. He hoped that the resumption of U.S. tests would persuade Moscow that it could not surpass the United States in nuclear weapons and that both sides would do better to agree on a permanent mutual ban on testing.

But after his 1963 American University speech on peace, Kennedy tried to raise the test ban again. To this end, Kennedy seized on Moscow's positive response to his speech by arranging for Averell Harriman, who had a long record of dealings with Moscow beginning in World War II as Franklin Roosevelt's ambassador, to head a negotiating delegation to Russia.

Because talk of some kind of Soviet-American rapprochement triggered fears that the United States might step back from its defense of

Western Europe and increase pressure in France and Germany to acquire nuclear arms, Kennedy mapped out a European trip that would calm NATO allies. His ten-day visit to Germany, Italy, and Ireland from June 23 to July 2, 1963, was a triumph of public diplomacy. In Germany, he assured audiences that American isolationism was long past. He urged NATO allies to increase their defense budgets. In West Berlin, where 60 percent of the city's population greeted Kennedy with chants of "*Kenne-dy*," "*Kenne-dy*," he denounced the Berlin wall that separated East and West Berlin and stemmed the flow of Germans and East Europeans from the communist East. To balance his Berlin remarks that attacked communism, Kennedy declared at the city's Free University that the West was open to reconciliation with the East.

The trip exhilarated Kennedy, who considered it the most successful day of his presidency, and made him keener than ever to work out a test ban with the Soviets. When Harriman and his delegation arrived in Moscow, Khrushchev greeted them by saying that he was eager for a relaxation of tensions and an agreement that reduced the risks of a nuclear war. But neither side wanted to be seen as taken advantage of by the other. Khrushchev was in trouble with his Kremlin associates for the setback in Cuba, and going into a reelection year, Kennedy could not be seen as too trusting of the Soviets. Where Kennedy wanted a comprehensive agreement that banned all nuclear testing, Khrushchev would only agree to a ban on atmospheric, outer space, and underwater tests, but not underground explosions. He feared that Moscow was too far behind the United States in weapons development to suspend all tests. The United States wanted comprehensive inspections, which the Soviets rejected. Yet in ten days, they reached agreement on a limited test ban with an escape clause that allowed either side to quit the treaty if one of them violated it with a banned test, or if a nonsignatory (China) tested a weapon that seemed to threaten either country's national security.

Fearful that his exclusion of the military chiefs and Republican senators from the Moscow negotiations would jeopardize its approval in the Senate, Kennedy appealed for public support in a televised speech in July. Reminding Americans that a nuclear war could produce unprecedented loss of life and devastation, Kennedy declared that the treaty represented "a shaft of light [that] cut into the darkness" by "bringing the forces of nuclear destruction under international control." With 80 percent of the country approving of the treaty and Kennedy more popular than ever, in September eighty senators voted for it. Where six months before 60 percent of Americans feared a war in which hydrogen bombs were used, the treaty reduced that number to 25 percent.

Although Kennedy had no interest in cozying up to Castro, he also saw relations with Cuba as a bar to better relations with Russia. After the resolution of the missile crisis, he told Khrushchev that "it is clearly in the interest of both sides that we reach agreement on how finally to dispose of the Cuban crisis." At the same time, however, he instructed his military chiefs to plan a future invasion of the island, and told Secretary McNamara to give such plans "the highest priority." Yet he was receptive to a report from New York lawyer James B. Donovan, who was in Cuba to negotiate the release of the Cuban exiles captured during the Bay of Pigs invasion, that Castro, who was angered by Khrushchev's cave-in to Kennedy, had expressed an interest in renewing official relations with the United States. In the summer of 1963, William Attwood, a former *Look* magazine editor who had become an adviser to America's U.N. delegation, assumed the role of a go-between with the U.N.'s Cuban representative.

At the same time, Jean Daniel, a French journalist scheduled to visit

Havana, met with Kennedy in Washington. The president expressed an interest in discussing Cuba and asked Daniel to see him again after his stay in Havana, saying, "Castro's reactions interest me." Attwood reported that Castro was open to secret conversations with an American envoy. Like Kennedy, Castro was mindful of the political tensions any rapprochement with Cuba would reduce. On November 12, Kennedy gave a speech in Miami that signaled the administration's interest in a fresh start in Cuban-American relations. Whether Kennedy could have worked out differences with Castro is an open question. As part of any new beginning, Castro wanted the U.S. to give up its Guantánamo naval base on the island, which would have provoked a harsh reaction against the Kennedy White House if he agreed to it.

While Cuba was an immediate daunting problem, U.S. involvement in Southeast Asia was growing and threatening to become a major source of domestic controversy. The Eisenhower administration's commitment to the defense of South Vietnam from Ho Chi Minh's communist North had become a Kennedy dilemma. All of Indochina, which included Laos and Cambodia, had been a Kennedy concern since his Senate years. By the time he had become president, the region was an East-West battleground, with Washington concerned about defeating communist insurgents fighting for control. While planners in the Kennedy administration struggled to come up with a way to preserve Indochina from a communist takeover, they worried about devoting resources to a fight over an area with marginal national security value to the United States. Because the Russians and the Chinese as well were reluctant to put resources into an uncertain civil war, Moscow, Peking, and Washington signed on to a neutrality agreement that put Laos aside.

But the same could not be arranged for Vietnam. When Averell Harriman, under instructions from Kennedy, secretly met with North

Vietnam's foreign minister in Geneva, Switzerland, to discuss peace, he "got absolutely nowhere." The alternative was to keep helping South Vietnam. Although Kennedy made clear to his advisers that he did not want to turn South Vietnam's fight against Viet Cong communist insurgents into an American combat operation, he was willing to expand the number of U.S. military advisers in the South from roughly eight hundred to sixteen thousand. By the spring of 1962, American military and aid officials in Saigon reported that we were turning the corner in Vietnam. Secretary of Defense McNamara declared after a trip to the South Vietnamese countryside that he had "seen nothing but progress and hopeful indications of further progress." One reporter described it as "a Gibraltar of optimism." Pressed by another reporter to be more truthful, McNamara replied, "Every quantitative measurement we have shows we're winning this war." The administration had introduced a Strategic Hamlet program in the countryside that U.S. embassy officials described as "little short of sensational." At Kennedy's direction, McNamara drew up a three-year plan for removing U.S. military forces from Vietnam by 1965 and cutting military assistance by 75 percent.

At the end of 1962, however, reports of poor South Vietnamese performance in the fighting, and complaints from journalists in Vietnam that the U.S. was fooling itself about progress in the war and about the popularity of Ngo Dinh Diem's government, forced Kennedy to reconsider the challenges there. Although Kennedy declared in his January 1963 State of the Union address that "the spear point of aggression has been blunted in Vietnam," he also acknowledged that it remained a point of "uncertainty." Still, he ordered McNamara to withdraw one thousand of America's military advisers from Vietnam by the end of the year. He also told Montana Democratic senator Mike Mansfield that he expected to withdraw from Vietnam after he was reelected in 1964. However, after Diem provoked a crisis with the majority Buddhists in Vietnam in the summer of 1963, Kennedy had to decide how to stabilize the country.

He found no help from a State Department expert and a marine general who gave diametrically different reports on Vietnam. "The two of you did visit the same country, didn't you?" he asked. A war of views also erupted in the press on what the United States should do—escalate or give up on Vietnam as a hopeless cause. Kennedy found a middle ground of sorts by deciding that Diem's continuing control of the government in Saigon promised nothing but instability, and therefore he should be ousted in a military coup. But he wished to be sure that it would not be blamed on the United States, especially if it failed. Events, however, were now beyond U.S. control, and when a coup occurred on November 1 and Diem was assassinated, Kennedy was pained by his death, saying, "It should not have ended like this." In a tape he made on November 4, he seemed to believe that the best future course for the United States was to get out of Vietnam as expeditiously as possible. As he left for a political visit to Texas on November 21, he sent a memo to a State Department official "to organize an in-depth study of every possible option we've got in Vietnam, including how to get out of there. We have to review this whole thing from the bottom to the top."

But events in Dallas, Texas, on November 22 ended Kennedy's presidency. Kennedy's assassination that day has generated a vast conspiracy literature, blaming U.S. Army chiefs, the CIA, the FBI, the Mafia, Cubans, Vietnamese, Vice President Lyndon Johnson, anti-Kennedy businessmen, and too many others to recount. To this day, a large plurality of the country believes that the conspiracy theorists have it right. Millions of Americans cannot accept that someone as inconsequential as Lee Harvey Oswald, the man official accounts describe as the sole killer, could possibly be the lone assassin. People don't want to believe that the world is so disordered that a ne'er-do-well like Oswald could have killed a president.

As for Kennedy's historical reputation, it remains exceptionally high. Despite being in office for only a thousand days, he is remembered as America's best recent president, exceeding the regard for Harry Truman, Dwight Eisenhower, Ronald Reagan, Bill Clinton, or Barack Obama. His assassination at the age of forty-six inflates the regard for him that comes from visions of what he might have accomplished in a second term. And the missteps of Kennedy's successors enhance his standing as a wise leader who towers above all the presidents since 1963.

That Kennedy holds such widespread regard after only a thousand days in office may have encouraged his successors to believe that presidential reputation rests less on what they achieve in office than their ability to create a reputation based on public relations skills. Because revelations about Kennedy's womanizing have not damaged his historical standing, it has encouraged other womanizers to believe that their behavior was not a deterrent to running for or serving in the White House. Moreover, Kennedy's legacy rests as much on image as substance. It has encouraged every presidential administration since 1963 to believe that regardless of what they did, including failed policies, they could enhance their public standing with behavior that makes them appear successful. And, of course, the importance of television and rhetoric in putting a halo over a president does more to make a positive impression than the reality of what an administration achieves; at least for a while. While no one can say that this is just the result of John Kennedy's affinity for beneficial appearances, he certainly made this an indispensable part of how future presidents believed they should behave.

CHAPTER 7

Lyndon B. Johnson

Flawed Giant

As with other vice presidents who unexpectedly assumed office like Theodore Roosevelt, Calvin Coolidge, and Harry Truman, Lyndon Johnson understood that his initial task was to convince Americans that he was ready to fulfill his predecessor's agenda. In his speech before a joint session of Congress five days after Kennedy's death, Johnson recounted Kennedy's goals and quoted his request to the country, "Let us begin." Johnson now declared, "Let us continue," urging Congress to pass Kennedy's stalled agenda—cutting taxes; approving Medicare, federal aid to education, and a civil rights law ending racial segregation in all places of public accommodation.

Johnson like Kennedy came to the presidency with a world of political experience. His father had served in the Texas lower house and in 1931 had arranged for Lyndon, who was teaching speech in Houston's Sam Houston High School, to become a congressional secretary to Texas congressman Richard Kleberg—a playboy from the Rio Grande Valley. Kleberg was a member of the wealthy King Ranch family that owned a huge spread in the Valley. He was also a self-indulgent patrician with little interest in government or working with the Roosevelt White House to end the Depression. He largely left the business of his office to Johnson, an avid supporter of FDR's New Deal.

In 1935, Johnson convinced House Speaker Sam Rayburn, a fellow Texan, to have FDR name him director of the Texas division of the National Youth Administration (NYA), an agency the White House had created to help young people develop job skills that could keep them off the unemployment rolls. Johnson quickly established himself as the best state director in the nation, so much so that Eleanor Roosevelt visited him in Austin to observe his methods. What made him special was his boldness in spending an occasional night at a black college, which, had it been known at the time in strict segregationist Texas, would have undermined his chances of ever running for public office. Johnson had a special regard for underdogs who wished to improve themselves; it was an extension of his own experience. Young black men who asked if they could become an engineer or an airline pilot especially touched Johnson's sense of injustice about the roadblock to a better life for people of color.

In 1937, when the congressman from the Tenth Congressional District that included Austin died, Johnson entered the special election vying with nine other older candidates for the seat. He ran an impressively energetic campaign, promising to support Franklin Roosevelt's effort to pack the Supreme Court with liberal New Deal advocates. When Johnson won, Roosevelt, who had been on a fishing trip in the Gulf of Mexico and was taking a train from Galveston to Texas A&M, where he was scheduled to give a speech, invited Johnson to join him on the train. Roosevelt asked what House committee Johnson would like to serve on, and he replied the Ways and Means or the House Rules committee. Because only senior members of the

House won appointment to those committees, Roosevelt laughed and suggested that Johnson serve on the House Naval Affairs committee. Johnson was agreeable, understanding that Roosevelt wanted a sure vote to help expand the navy as a deterrent to Japanese aggression in the Pacific. Roosevelt told an aide that Johnson was the sort of ambitious politician from the Southwest, which would grow more important in America's future politics, who could one day become president.

Johnson's House career was notable for its loyalty to Roosevelt, whom he admired for his political skills and commitment to struggling Americans. In 1940, Johnson supported the president's requests for an unprecedented peacetime draft and a third term. After the Pearl Harbor attack in December 1941, Johnson used his political contacts to join the navy as a lieutenant commander. Eager to support the country's fighting spirit and build a war record that would serve his political ambitions, he persuaded Roosevelt to send him on a fact-finding mission to the southwest Pacific, where he convinced General Douglas MacArthur to let him go on a B-24 bombing raid against the Japanese in New Guinea. One of three bombers, which he initially boarded and then left for a seat on a second plane, was shot down with all aboard killed. In a swap with MacArthur, he promised to urge Roosevelt to provide more resources for the Pacific War, in return for which the general awarded him a Silver Star. Johnson's opponents described it as the least deserved and most talked about medal in World War II.

Johnson's decoration was insufficient to save him from a defeat by Texas governor Pappy "Pass the Biscuits" O'Daniel in a 1941 Democratic primary for a U.S. Senate seat, done in by ballot stuffing by O'Daniel supporters in the liquor lobby. When Johnson ran again for a Senate seat in 1948, he made sure his own side manipulated the final primary tally. Running against Coke Stevenson, another popular Texas governor, Johnson faced a tough primary fight for the Democratic nomination, which was tantamount to winning a U.S. Senate seat, as no Republican was going to defeat a Democrat in a statewide election that year. With the primary essentially deadlocked, Johnson's backers went into the Rio Grande Valley town of Alice, Texas, where they added two hundred votes to the tally, giving Johnson an eighty-seven-vote lead out of the million that were cast. Although he won a court fight against Stevenson to keep the lead, the result opened Johnson to ridicule, earning him the nickname Landslide Lyndon. In Texas, people joked that a little boy complained that when his father came back from the grave to vote for Lyndon Johnson in the election, he never came by to say hello to him.

As a senator, Johnson was less interested in committee assignments than in becoming a Democratic Party leader, and he quickly established himself as a larger-than-life character with an extraordinary understanding of Washington politics, or maybe more to the point, an exceptional grasp of people's strengths and limits. The historian Arthur Schlesinger described Johnson as a character Mark Twain and William Faulkner could have invented, and Schlesinger recalled a meeting with him in which Johnson described every member of the Senate—"his drinking habits, his sex life, his intellectual capacity," and the best way to manage him, including Joe McCarthy, whom he did so much to bring down.

In 1951, after two years in the upper house, he told a journalist interviewing him not to write an article about congressional leaders but "a whole big article on just me alone." "What would the pitch of an article on you be?" the journalist asked. "That you might be a Vice-Presidential candidate for 1952?" "Vice President hell!" Johnson replied. "Who wants that? . . . President! That's the angle you want to write about me." To move toward a presidential run, Johnson served on the Armed Services Committee, which carried special influence in the midst of the Korean War. After serving as Democratic Party whip and minority leader, Johnson became the party's majority leader in January 1955 at the age of forty-six, the youngest man ever to assume that position.

His energy became legendary. A journalist reported that "rest and relaxation" were "painful" to him. Someone described him like Napoleon as "a tornado in pants," working twelve- , fourteen- , and sixteen-hour days. In Washington, a reporter said, "Energy in its purest political form is expressed in the letters E = LBJ." His whirlwind schedule caught up with him in 1955 when he suffered a massive heart attack. Although he came close to dying, he recovered and soon resumed his breathtaking pace and run for the presidency. FDR's disability and Eisenhower's heart attacks muted any concerns voters might have had about Johnson's health, though he took pains to assure people of his physical well-being.

But if he were to win the Democratic presidential nomination, he needed to demonstrate not just control of his party and a return to robust health but national leadership. As late as the 1950s, the curse of the Civil War still hung over the Democratic South. No one from that region had come close to running for, let alone winning, the presidency.

Johnson saw a route to the presidency through accomplishments as a national security expert and a progressive on race relations. In 1957, after Sputnik, Washington put a premium on competing in the space race. Johnson made it a top priority in cooperation with Eisenhower's Republican administration. He sponsored a bill creating a National Aeronautics and Space Administration. Mindful of the imbalance in defense spending that would result from putting the agency under one of the military branches, Johnson arranged for civilian control that encouraged the belief in space as an area of scientific advance rather than military competition. It was an act of statesmanship worthy of a president (unlike Trump, who wants to weaponize space).

The space agency gave Johnson credentials as a masterful bipartisan national legislator. But nothing was better calculated to advance his standing as a national politician than the support of a Deep South senator for civil rights legislation. By 1957, equal treatment for African Americans under the law had become a compelling national issue. In February, *Time* had put Martin Luther King on its cover and praised him for leading a nonviolent movement seeking justifiable social change. Since no major civil rights legislation had passed Congress since 1875, such a law was certain to command widespread attention. But such a law impressed Johnson as not only good personal politics but also a necessary advance of social justice. Whatever his prejudice against African Americans, which seemed inescapable for a majority of southerners growing up below the Mason-Dixon line, he understood that they had been treated unfairly and held back from achieving prosperity and fulfilling their life's ambitions. He also understood that as long as segregation existed, it not only separated the races across the South but also separated the South from the rest of the nation. A racially integrated South would also make the region a more equal partner with the North and the West, and increase its economic opportunities and general prosperity. Not the least, however, it would make the South once again a major part of the national political conversation.

Johnson understood that passing a civil rights bill in 1957 could only be done if it were a measured law that did not end segregation across the South but instead addressed the principal issue of voting rights. When the law passed, it provoked contrasting reactions. Critics said it was no more than a sham law, "a mere fakery," that promised much and gave little. Eisenhower's deputy attorney general compared the law to "handing a policeman a gun with no bullets in it." Two years after the law passed, black voting across the South was constricted as ever. But it cast a light on the path ahead. For the first time in almost a century, it opened the way to future consideration of civil rights legislation that could right historic wrongs. Legislative remedies to southern segregation had become a realistic possibility.

Yet none of this made Johnson a front-runner for his party's presidential nomination. Although there were only eight state primaries in 1960 and the party bosses liked Johnson, he faced tough competition from fellow senators John Kennedy and Minnesota's Hubert Humphrey, a leading voice on civil rights. Moreover, Johnson mistakenly assumed that his record of achievement as majority leader relieved him of the need to enter the primaries or to explain his growing wealth, which never came from his congressional salaries. His ownership or, more accurately, Lady Bird Johnson's lucrative ownership of radio and TV stations in Austin, Texas, was understandably seen as the product of his political influence. In addition, for all his brilliance as a politician, Johnson lacked Kennedy's charm or charisma. Johnson supposedly asked Dean Acheson, "Why don't people like me?" "Because," Acheson bluntly replied, "you are not a very likeable man."

Johnson believed that Kennedy's youth, Catholicism, and health, and Humphrey's ultraliberalism, would bar them from the nomination. He said about Kennedy: That "kid needs a little gray in his hair," and called him a "playboy" and a "lightweight." And he attacked Humphrey as a "liberal bomb thrower," someone too far to the left to lead the nation. But when Kennedy won the nomination,

Johnson received the nod for the vice presidency. Although Kennedy's brother Bobby and Johnson disliked each other and Bobby lobbied against the decision, Kennedy understood that he badly needed a southerner on the ticket to help him overcome southern bias against a northeastern Catholic. It was a smart move, as Johnson helped put Kennedy over the top in Texas and gave him a boost from having so experienced a politician as second-in-command; it was vital in an exceptionally close election.

Johnson, who could never stand being second fiddle, hated being vice president, though he took solace from the hope that, like Nixon, eight years as the understudy could facilitate a presidential bid in 1968, when Johnson would be only sixty. And so, when Lee Harvey Oswald killed Kennedy in November 1963, Johnson instantly became president. To blunt dangerous speculation that Moscow had arranged Kennedy's killing, which an Oswald visit to Russia and marriage to a Russian woman seemed to suggest; and to shield himself from accusations that his ambition had made him part of a conspiracy to replace Kennedy; and to allay his own suspicions about the possible culprits in the American military and CIA, Johnson established the Warren Commission, headed by Chief Justice Earl Warren, to probe the assassination. Though the commission's conclusion that Oswald was the sole killer put most of the suspicions aside, it never decisively ended the belief in a conspiracy. Nor is it clear that it ever entirely convinced Johnson of Oswald's culpability, but it reduced speculation of a Soviet part in killing the president. More important, the commission's report dispelled talk of a war with Moscow.

Because few people in the country knew much, if anything, about Lyndon Johnson, and because 70 percent of Americans expressed doubts about how the country would "carry on without" Kennedy, Johnson saw his initial challenge as president to restore confidence in the nation's capacity to move forward in both domestic and foreign affairs. His speech to the joint congressional session on November 27 immediately signaled that there would be no pause in advancing the national interest. Johnson relied on Kennedy's brilliant speechwriter, Ted Sorensen, to craft rhetoric of hope and stability. He told the country that instead of "uncertainty and doubt . . . from the brutal loss of our leader, we will derive not weakness, but strength; that we can and will act and act now." (It was reminiscent of FDR's first Inaugural Address: "This nation is asking for action, and action now.") It was then that Johnson urged the country to continue the pursuit of Kennedy's congressional agenda and the search for world peace. His twenty-five-minute speech received thirty-four bursts of prolonged applause. Most fateful of all at the time was a private conversation between Henry Cabot Lodge and Johnson in his first week as president, in which he promised Lodge not to lose the fight in Kennedy's expanded war in Vietnam.

But Johnson saw domestic reform as more urgent, mostly because his greater interest and expertise were in domestic affairs. He signaled his priorities by pushing first for Kennedy's tax reform, cutting the highest rate from 91 to 70 percent. Partly on a wave of sentiment to honor Kennedy's memory, the tax bill passed Congress at the end of February 1964.

While Johnson was ready to press for a civil rights bill next, he made clear that he had ambitions running far beyond JFK's four reforms. At the University of Michigan's commencement in May 1964, he unveiled his determination to eclipse all earlier presidents with an unprecedented program of domestic advance: It was the application of Johnson's grandiosity to the political/social arena. Using the speech to provide a label for his administration, he shunned the "Good Society" suggested by aides to call it "The Great Society."

But he believed that labels were only compelling if they sat atop a popular, realizable agenda: He said we have the opportunity to use the country's past achievements "to move not only toward the rich society and the powerful society, but upward to the Great Society." He intended to fight a war on poverty, rebuild America's cities with modern systems of transportation and housing, preserve and expand "America the beautiful" by cleaning and protecting the environment, rebuild the country's educational institutions to promote a love of learning that would help raise youngsters out of poverty, and ensure equality of treatment and opportunity for every American regardless of race, creed, or belief. The speech before eighty thousand people instantly became the hallmark of Johnson's administration.

On racial issues, Johnson was an American Janus: he had his stereotypes of minorities, particularly about blacks and Hispanics. In private he could use the N-word and talk about African Americans as lazy breeders who liked to live off the public dole, or Mexican Americans who didn't care about learning English and didn't mind exploiting hard-working taxpayers. Yet Johnson could rise above his gross prejudices to champion government programs intended to improve the lives of minorities and benefit the entire nation, especially in his native South. He saw segregation as a southern curse that not only held back blacks but the entire region. He was determined to pass Kennedy's civil rights bill and he understood the historical importance of his action, saying, "I'm going to be the President who finishes what Lincoln began." As he told black leaders, "This bill is going to be enacted because justice and morality demand it."

In the spring of 1964, as news of Johnson's push for civil rights became public knowledge, a Gallup poll recorded a 57 percent approval for the president's leadership on this hot-button issue. As the bill moved through Congress, Johnson followed every twist and turn, speaking constantly on the telephone to members of both houses to pressure them into support. At the same time, he made repeated public appeals, telling the press after the House passed the bill that he expected a Senate filibuster from southern senators and that he was "not going to put anything on that floor until this is done." He courted southern senators by urging them to understand that they would do better with a bill from a fellow southerner than from a more militant liberal. He also made special efforts to bring Republican senators on board, promising them favors and shared glory for supporting the bill. Everett Dirksen, the Republican leader in the Senate who enjoyed the courting, closed the Senate discussion on cloture by quoting Victor Hugo: "Stronger than all the armies is an idea whose time has come." When the bill became law in July, Johnson had a televised signing at the White House before a hundred dignitaries, explaining that the blessings of liberty, which the founding fathers had enshrined in the Constitution, were now extended to all Americans.

Johnson was mindful of the impact his success in steering the civil rights law through Congress would have on the election. He was eager to shed the mantle of Kennedy's successor and become president in his own right by winning a decisive victory in the 1964 presidential campaign. To assure that a victory would be seen as his alone and in no way tied to his association with the Kennedys, he rejected suggestions that Bobby Kennedy be the vice presidential nominee. Yet fearful that a filmed tribute to JFK might spark a movement at the convention to elevate Bobby, Johnson arranged to delay the showing of the JFK tribute until the end of the convention, after Minnesota senator Hubert Humphrey had been chosen for the post.

The election itself turned into a Democratic rout of the Republicans. Angered by Johnson's talk about a Great Society and a war on poverty, all of which promised to increase the number and extent of federal government programs, the Republicans rejected the candidacy of New York's moderate governor Nelson Rockefeller by nominating conservative Arizona senator Barry Goldwater. Goldwater was notable for his antigovernment Hoover conservatism that included threats to Roosevelt's welfare state, especially Social Security, the TVA, and the graduated income tax. Moreover, he had distinguished himself as a militant anti-communist who had declared that we should think about withdrawing recognition of the Soviet Union and lobbing a nuclear weapon into the men's room of the Kremlin. Mindful of how radical Goldwater seemed to most Americans, the Johnson campaign, led by press secretary Bill Moyers, developed the most famous negative campaign ad in presidential history—the "Daisy Field" ad. The brief video pictured a pretty young girl in a field of daisies, picking the petals off a flower while the voiceover counted down from ten to zero when a mushroom cloud appeared in the background with the legend "Vote for President Johnson. . . . The stakes are too high for you to stay home." Although the ad made a strong impression on voters, it became so controversial that it only ran once.

Despite the widespread judgment that Goldwater's militant conservatism would cost him the election, Johnson, remembering his close calls in 1941 and 1948, took nothing for granted. He was especially worried that Goldwater's tough talk about defeating communism would give him an advantage with voters, especially in the fight to save South Vietnam from Viet Cong guerrillas. Consequently, in August 1964, when a North Vietnamese torpedo boat attacked a U.S. destroyer in the Tonkin Gulf, Johnson wanted to show his resolve to combat the communist threat. Initially, Johnson wrote the attack off as a random incident of too little consequence to respond. But when a second attack allegedly occurred, he felt he had to strike back.

Persuaded by confirming reports from the U.S. military command in the Pacific, he asked Congress for a resolution giving him backing to respond. Remembering Truman's difficulties with Congress and public opinion after the Korean War had become a stalemate, Johnson wanted to be sure that he had clear support for any military action. He prepared the ground with a nationally televised speech and a request that Congress give him sanction to defend U.S. interests across Southeast Asia. After the resolution received unanimous support in the House and only two dissenting votes in the Senate, Johnson said privately that he loved the resolution: It was "like grandma's nightshirt—it covered everything."

Johnson's Tonkin Gulf resolution opened the way to a U.S. military disaster, but it gave Johnson another edge in a one-sided election. In September 1964, more than eleven thousand psychiatrists declared Goldwater emotionally unfit to be president. Although it added to the general belief that Goldwater lacked the temperament to be a competent chief executive, it generated the American Psychiatric Association's "Goldwater rule" that condemned psychiatric evaluations of public figures as unfair unless the therapist had direct contact with the individual under scrutiny. Yet when bumper stickers supporting Goldwater appeared saying "In Your Heart You Know He's Right," Democrats responded with "Yes, far right," "In your heart you know he might," and "In your gut, you know he's nuts." The verbal assault on Goldwater stands as a character assassination that opened the way to similar attacks on other politicians, adding to the public belief that politics was a dirty business.

In November, Johnson scored one of the great landslide victories in U.S. history, winning 61 percent of the popular vote and forty-four states to Goldwater's six, as well as his party's supermajorities in both houses of Congress.

Johnson understood that his victory gave him a mandate to enact his Great Society program. But he also knew that he had limited time to manage Congress. "I've watched the Congress . . . for more than forty years," he told Eric Goldman, the Princeton historian who had become a White House adviser, "and I've never seen a Congress that didn't eventually take the measure of the president it was dealing with."

Johnson quickly set to work to push a host of reforms through Congress, including Medicare and federal aid to education—both left over from the Kennedy presidency. Getting Medicare passed meant getting a bill by Arkansas congressman Wilbur Mills, who chaired the House Ways and Means Committee. A "prissy, prim and proper man," as Johnson called him, Mills was a deficit hawk who feared a Medicare law would swell the federal debt. But because the idea of health insurance for the elderly had become irresistible, Congress passed the bill in July 1965. Despite the vast increase in the costs of Medicare and Medicaid, its sister program for poor Americans, federally funded health insurance has become a permanent fixture of the government, with periodic talk of revisions that can eventually rein in the costs.

Along with Medicare, Johnson was avid to make the federal government a principal influence on the country's educational systems, which were seeing a crush of baby-boom-generation students flooding into public schools. He called education "the guardian genius of our democracy" and said that "nothing matters more to the future of our country." He believed that expanding opportunity and spreading prosperity depended on upgrading American education at all levels. The Elementary and Secondary Education Act faced sharp challenges in Congress, especially from Republicans and southern

Democrats resistant to expanding government influence. But Johnson, with his keen feel for how to win majority support, and arm-twisting tactics, drove the bill through Congress.

Typical of his technique in managing congressional sensitivities was his outreach to Massachusetts Republican congressman Silvio Conte. When Johnson called him, Conte later said, "he damn near collapsed right on the spot . . . It's the only time since I have been in Congress that a president called me. I will never forget it." Jake Pickle, the Democratic congressman who replaced Johnson in the tenth Texas district, said, "It would be nothing for [Johnson] to talk to fifteen, twenty, or thirty different congressmen or senators during a day." Johnson told his staff that the most important job they have is the day-to-day contact with members of Congress, and administration support for what these elected officials viewed as essential to their constituents' needs and their voter appeal.

All of Johnson's efforts paid off handsomely in helping him put across 207 reforms, including a new immigration statute that ended the race- and ethnicity-based 1924 National Origins Formula that had barred so many southern and eastern European migrants from coming to the United States. In addition, Johnson presided over the creation of departments of transportation and housing and urban development, as well as a host of measures protecting the environment, especially clean air and clean water; and consumer protections such as safe tires, foods, and medicines; and traffic safety to reduce the number of road fatalities. Nor did he neglect the country's cultural affairs, establishing endowments for the arts and the humanities, and a Freedom of Information Act (FOIA) to assure timely access to historical documents. As a symbol of what Johnson thought would be an appropriate endnote to the rush of federal agencies and Great

Society programs, he made the last official act of his presidency in January 1969 the naming of a national park in Alaska for Franklin D. Roosevelt—the architect of the welfare state.

No domestic action during Johnson's five-plus years in the White House was more consequential than the 1965 Voting Rights Act. Johnson was not eager to press for any more civil rights laws that would further compel changes on the South. He hoped that the 1964 law would open the way to increased opportunity for black voting. But with only 6 percent of blacks registered to vote in Mississippi and 19 percent in Alabama, it was a large challenge to overcome. And when Johnson showed no signs of moving on the issue, Martin Luther King took up the cause in Selma, Alabama, where less than 1 percent of blacks were on the voter rolls. A series of marches beginning in Selma generated national attention when state and local law enforcement officials used force to break them up. Convinced that the 1964 law was insufficient to compel the states to give blacks the ballot, Johnson and House members now put a voting rights bill before Congress.

To compel quick action on the issue before more violence occurred, Johnson federalized the Alabama National Guard, putting it directly under the president's command to defend King and a national gathering of marchers walking from Selma to Montgomery, the state capital. When King asked historians from across the country to join in the final day of the march to witness a landmark moment in the country's experience, I was lucky enough to be one of fifty or so chosen to see history in the making. I have the unforgettable image of our walk through the black neighborhood, where elderly women stood on their porches waving handkerchiefs at us and crying. I cannot forget the sight of federalized guardsman whose hostility to us was controlled but palpable. Nor can I forget the speech Martin Luther King made in the city center to the huge gathering supporting the demand for congressional action.

To break through the controversy, Johnson went before Congress to press the case for the voting rights law. It was his most moving and greatest speech. Comparing the marchers to the patriots who fought British rule at Lexington and Concord, he described the black struggle to vote as a battle by "American Negroes to secure for themselves the full blessings of American life. Their cause must be our cause too," he said. "Because it's not just Negroes, but really it's all of us, who must overcome the crippling legacy of bigotry and injustice. And"—Johnson paused, raising his arms for emphasis—"we shall overcome," using the anthem of the civil rights movement. That August, the Voting Rights Acts passed in both houses of Congress by lopsided margins. The law's immediate effect was evident in 1968 when black registration across the eleven former Confederate states averaged 62 percent, demonstrating that the only thing that had stood in the way of black voting had been impossible literacy tests and other impediments to keep blacks away from the polls. By 1980, the nation could count ten million black voters, only 7 percent less than the proportion of voting-age whites.

At the same time Johnson worked to build a Great Society, he stumbled into an unwinnable war in Vietnam. Mindful, like Franklin Roosevelt, that any conflict costing the country blood and treasure needed to rest on a stable national consensus, Johnson led the country into this jungle war by stealth. Believing that the Tonkin Gulf resolution gave him sufficient backing for executive action without additional congressional approval, in March 1965 Johnson launched an air campaign, "Rolling Thunder," against North Vietnam after the Viet Cong staged an attack on an American military base at Pleiku in the Vietnamese highlands that killed eight advisers.

In April, Johnson responded to mounting criticism of his policy with a billion-dollar development program for Vietnam to which "Ho will never be able to say no," or so Johnson believed. But Ho rejected the offer, convinced that his people could outlast the United States in a long war.

By July, with evidence that the air raids were not deterring the insurgents, Johnson agreed to send a hundred thousand ground troops to fight in Vietnam. Because he did not want to draw attention to his escalation of the U.S. commitment to the fighting, he announced the dispatch of the troops at a press conference in which he also revealed a decision to nominate Abe Fortas, his longtime attorney and friend, to the Supreme Court. A warning from Vice President Hubert Humphrey that it was a mistake to involve the country in a guerrilla war without a firmer public commitment did nothing to alter Johnson's decision. That summer only 48 percent of an opinion survey favored "sending a large number of American troops to help save Vietnam."

By the end of 1965, with no clear resolution of the conflict, the Joint Chiefs persuaded Johnson to send another 120,000 troops to Vietnam. To mute the decision and not add to mounting domestic opposition, he told the chiefs that he would announce increases of ten thousand each month. But a significant number of Americans were not fooled, especially on college campuses where young men faced the prospect of being drafted and sent to fight an unpopular war. When Johnson spoke of light at the end of the tunnel, critics said that the light could be from an onrushing train. Johnson now dug in his heels against war opponents, complaining that they were serving the communists and might in fact be part of a gigantic communist conspiracy. The communist way of thinking had infected everyone around him, he told press secretary Bill Moyers.

His insistent description of progress in Vietnam and complaints that critics were undermining the war effort triggered a credibility gap. As casualties began to mount in the war and demonstrators outside the White House chanted, "Hey, hey, LBJ, how many kids did you kill today?" Johnson became the object of ridicule: "How do you know when Lyndon Johnson is telling the truth?" comedians asked. "When he pulls his ear lobe, scratches his chin, he's telling the truth. When he begins to move his lips, you know he's lying." The popular journalist Hugh Sidey said that to Johnson "the shortest distance between two points was a tunnel." A culture gap now opened between Johnson and many of the country's academics and intellectuals. One said, "I look at that Texas cowhand and listen to him mangle the language and I say, 'No, dammit, go fight your own war.'" Johnson privately described these critics as "snobs," "sons of bitches," and close to being "traitors."

But he wouldn't say these things in public. He understood that such coarse language would simply deepen the antagonism to him and sully the presidential office. With talk of his impeachment rising in Congress and the press, he resisted intensifying hostility to himself by public attacks on opponents.

In August 1967, R. W. "Johnny" Apple, the *New York Times* Saigon bureau chief, published a front-page story saying that the war in Vietnam was a stalemate. Despite four hundred thousand U.S. troops and an army of seven hundred thousand South Vietnamese, Apple described victory as neither "close at hand" nor within reach. He quoted American officers who estimated the war might go on for decades. Moreover, he described the South Vietnamese government as likely to crumple once the U.S. military prop was removed. Privately, Johnson called Apple a "communist" and "a threat to national security." One of Apple's military sources thought that the United

States needed to "find a dignified way of getting out." But all this remained hidden from public view.

Because "losing" was never a word in Johnson's vocabulary, he continued to insist that there was light at the end of the tunnel, or corners were being turned, in the metaphors of the day; at least until the 1968 New Year or Tet Offensive by the Viet Cong and North Vietnamese. Even before the new round of communist aggression, U.S. public opinion had turned: 67 percent of a Harris poll disapproved of Johnson's handling of the war and 71 percent supported a negotiated settlement "as quickly as possible." Forty-six percent of Americans believed it was a mistake to have become involved in the conflict. Privately, war protesters were enraging Johnson. When a group of reporters pressed him to explain why we were in Vietnam, he "unzipped his fly, drew out his substantial organ, and declared: 'This is why!'" Fortunately, Johnson's crudeness did not reach the public.

Frustration and anguish over Vietnam was now taking a toll on people around Johnson. His defense secretary Robert McNamara seemed near physical collapse. Johnson thought him so distraught that he might take his own life. Johnson now pushed him out of the administration, making him president of the World Bank. When Vice President Hubert Humphrey returned from a visit to Vietnam, he told Johnson that they were involved in a lost cause: "We're murdering civilians by the thousands and our boys are dying in rotten jungles—for what? A corrupt, selfish government that has no feeling and no morality." Johnson told Humphrey not to repeat any of this. As Humphrey reported on his trip to the National Security Council, Johnson pushed a note across the table: "Make it short, make it sweet, and then shut up and sit down."

But Johnson could sustain the illusion of progress in the war for only so long. As the New Year began, he declared in his State of the Union message that "America will persevere," and when Hanoi was ready to talk peace and give up aggression, we would be eager to respond. But on January 30–31, the Viet Cong and North Vietnamese unleashed their surprisingly ferocious offensive across South Vietnam, attacking provincial capitals and five of its six largest cities. They penetrated the American embassy in Saigon and captured the ancient capital of Hue, which they held for almost four weeks. Despite the amazing statistic of more U.S. bombs dropped on Vietnam than U.S. air attacks in all theaters of World War II, talk of progress in the fighting, and heavy communist losses in the 1968 Tet offensive, the war was far from over. Although the communists could not claim a military victory from Tet, they had achieved a psychological one. Initially, the offensive produced a "rally" effect on American public opinion, strengthening the resolve to win in Vietnam.

But it was a temporary surge that faded by March. When South Vietnam's national police chief was shown on television executing a bound prisoner, the public reaction was one of horror that the United States was sponsoring such brutality. When CBS News anchor Walter Cronkite, the man labeled "the nation's most trusted person," described the war as mired in a stalemate, Johnson said, "If I've lost Cronkite, I've lost Middle America." Public support for the war now plunged to new lows: 49 percent of the country thought it had been a mistake to become so involved in Vietnam; 69 percent wanted the administration to announce a phase-out plan; 65 percent feared that the war could go on for at least two more years or longer; and 63 percent now disapproved of Johnson's handling of the war.

Despite his public rhetoric about persevering, Johnson knew that support for the war was so fragile that he risked domestic upheaval if he did not create hope of an end to the fighting. He told some aides,

"We have no support for the war." As a consequence, on March 31, he spoke to the nation about "Steps to Limit the War in Vietnam." He began his speech by saying, "Tonight I want to speak to you of peace in Vietnam and Southeast Asia." He then announced that we would stop the bombing of North Vietnam except for immediately north of the DMZ along the seventeenth parallel, and urged once again that Hanoi join us at the peace table.

Because riots in inner-city black ghettoes had underscored a division in American society between economic classes, he wanted to return the country's focus to his war on poverty and building a Great Society. But that would mean winning another presidential term, and in the current political climate, he saw it as more than unlikely. And not just because of Vietnam, but also because Johnson had lost the trust of the public. A member of his party said that faith in the government "had all but perished in the wake of a ruthless President who manipulates the rights of American citizens to know the truth about their government." In March, *New York Times* columnist James Reston decried the "poisonous mood" in Washington created by a president obsessed with his personal advantage.

In response to the decline of public support, Johnson had the good sense to announce at the close of his March 31 address that he wouldn't run again. Although seven months remained in Johnson's presidency, it was no more than a holding period both in Vietnam, where the fighting continued, and domestic affairs. It was a tragic end to a mixed-record presidency.

The Johnson presidency altered the country's political landscape. Where Johnson's landslide victory in 1964 spurred talk of the demise of the Republican Party, his four-year term revived the fortunes of his conservative opponents, and fueled the political ambitions of men and women who saw federal government overreach in both domestic and foreign affairs and decried the new public thinking's untrustworthiness of government. To be sure, Johnson's Great Society programs made America a much more humane society, especially for African Americans, but its association with Johnson made future domestic reforms more difficult to achieve.

Johnson's deceitfulness on foreign affairs that surpassed that of TR and FDR in particularly destructive ways opened the way to the mendacity of Presidents Richard Nixon and Ronald Reagan.

His term of office also provided a powerful reminder of how any unpopular action abroad could undermine a president's public appeal, or how essential it was to hold public backing for any initiative that cost the country blood and treasure. Johnson's Great Society gave conservatives fresh ammunition against presidential overreach, but it also put in place social programs that could not be cast aside without public recriminations.

CHAPTER 8

Richard M. Nixon

America in Crisis

Johnson's decision not to run again opened the way for other Democrats to seek the presidency. By June 1968, the party's front-runner was Robert Kennedy, JFK's brother, former attorney general and now senator from New York. Winning the California primary largely assured his nomination, though it will always remain uncertain because he was shot and killed by Sirhan B. Sirhan, a Palestinian migrant to the United States who saw Kennedy as an advocate of Israel and an enemy of Palestinian rights. At the Democratic convention that summer in Chicago, marked by street riots protesting America's continuing war in Vietnam, the party nominated Hubert H. Humphrey, former Minnesota senator and Johnson vice president who, despite dissent from Johnson's Vietnam policy, was identified with the unpopular president and his failing war.

Humphrey's opponent was Richard Nixon, whose service as a congressman, senator, and vice president made him readily recognizable. It was surprising that in a time of considerable domestic turmoil—riots in inner cities, marches and violent opposition to the

Vietnam War, when a French travel agent advertised "See America While It Lasts"—that the country would turn to two of its most familiar political figures as possible successors to Johnson. It spoke perhaps to the eagerness among many for some reassurance that the nation could sustain its system of government.

Richard Nixon could not measure up to the test of character usually required of a presidential candidate: He had a reputation as "Tricky Dick," someone who had lied to the public in his runs for the House and the Senate. And like Joe McCarthy, he was notorious for a history of character assassination, exceeding the underhandedness of LBJ. But his long career in national politics could help him restore public order. To begin with, he was seen as an ordinary American. He was born and grew up in Southern California where he attended public schools and Whittier College, a school with four hundred students twelve miles east of Los Angeles, and close enough to his home where he could live and save money on dormitory fees. He excelled in his studies, debating, and school politics, winning election as student body president in his junior year. In 1934, at age twenty-one, he graduated and won a scholarship to Duke University School of Law. Despite a fine record at Duke, which made him third in his class at graduation in 1937, he could not find a position in a distinguished law firm while the Depression continued to beset the country. Instead, he returned to Southern California, where he took a job with a local law firm.

Although he became a partner in the firm in 1939, he was never keenly interested in law practice. After the United States entered World War II in December 1941, Nixon, following fourteen months in Washington at the Office of Price Administration, joined the navy, where he served until September 1945, when he accepted an invitation to run in 1946 as the Republican nominee for a House seat from

California's twelfth district. Against the backdrop of strikes and economic dislocation that had put Truman and the Democrats on the defensive, it was a good year for Republican candidates. Nixon's campaign against Jerry Voorhis, a five-term New Deal Democrat, was an exercise in scaremongering about the rise of big government under the Democrats and the postwar communist threat. Backed by big oil and conservative newspapers, Nixon, despite denunciations by opponents that he played fast and loose with the truth and was essentially a ruthless politician who identified himself with the common man while preparing to serve corporate interests, won a decisive victory.

It was the start of Nixon's almost thirty-year political career. After two terms in the House, he had gained national recognition serving on the Un-American Activities Committee (HUAC) as a vocal advocate of investigating Alger Hiss, a former State Department employee and Soviet agent. Nixon's campaign against Hiss was not simply a way to advance his political career and punish Hiss for betraying the United States, it was also a vehicle for retaliating against Northeast elitists and establishment figures like Hiss whom he saw as contemptuous of him.

In 1950, Nixon capitalized on his newfound public standing to run for an open Senate seat from California against Democratic candidate Helen Gahagan Douglas, a three-term House member, the wife of Hollywood movie star Melvyn Douglas, and a notable liberal friend of Eleanor Roosevelt's. Like Hiss, she had an elite Northeast pedigree. Calling the election a contest between "freedom and state socialism," Nixon declared Douglas an ally of Representative Vito Marcantonio, an avowed friend of the Communist Party, and distributed five hundred thousand pink sheets across California calling her the "pink lady" and saying that her House votes aligned her with

Marcantonio and made her an ally of leftist subversives. The Nixon campaign put up billboards across the state describing Nixon as "On Guard for America." At a time when Mao Tse-tung's Communist Party had taken over China and the United States was locked in war on the Korean peninsula against communist aggression, Nixon's appeal resonated powerfully with voters. He defeated Douglas in the election by nineteen points, the largest margin of victory of any Senate candidate in the country.

Less than two years into Nixon's Senate term, Eisenhower chose him as his vice presidential running mate. He was a counterweight to Ike's reputation as a moderate and gave the Republicans standing as the defenders of American values. Like Warren G. Harding in 1920, the Eisenhower campaign emphasized "Americanism."

But the campaign temporarily stumbled in September when the columnist Drew Pearson reported that rich donors had set up a secret fund for Nixon's family that allowed them to live beyond their earnings. Under prodding from Eisenhower, Nixon agreed to address the charge in a nationally televised response. An audience of sixty million people—the largest in history to that point—watched. Nixon gave a masterful performance. He came across to Americans as a regular guy with a nice family, explaining that the $18,000 in the fund was for campaign expenses he did not wish to charge taxpayers for, and not for a lavish lifestyle. He gave a full accounting of his family's assets and expenses, saying that his wife did not have a mink coat, the mark of middle-class affluence at the time, and wore a plain cloth coat. He struck an especially winning note with voters when he reported that someone had sent his two young daughters a cocker spaniel they had named Checkers—hence the later references to this as the Checkers Speech—and that his daughters loved the dog and they would not give him up. The speech was a great success; it was powerful TV theater and ushered in the age of political TV that John Kennedy, Ronald Reagan, and others have used so effectively to sell themselves to the public.

In the campaign, Nixon became the principal voice of the opposition. Because Ike was seen as a moderate who appealed to the political center, Nixon became the Republican "hatchet man," attacking the Truman administration's corruption and policy of "cowardly containment." He described Adlai Stevenson as a spineless dupe deceived by communist trickery. "Nothing would please the Kremlin more than a Stevenson presidency," he said. He appealed to the country's exaggerated fears about communists in the government and in their midst. With the Korean War stalemated and threats of Soviet aggression or subversion in Europe and Latin America, Nixon had a receptive audience that helped give the Eisenhower-Nixon ticket a resounding victory.

During his eight years as vice president, Nixon continued to represent the tough side of the Eisenhower administration, making a mark with his well-publicized 1958 confrontation with anti-American rioters in Caracas, Venezuela, and his 1959 "kitchen debate" with Nikita Khrushchev in Moscow. Eisenhower, Nixon claimed, was saving the United States from Democratic plans to socialize America. It was all part of what Nixon called "the international Communist conspiracy." Adlai Stevenson described Nixon's language as "white collar McCarthyism."

Nixon's notoriety as vice president opened the way for the then-unusual occurrence of a sitting VP winning the nomination to run for president. But Eisenhower undermined him when he responded to queries about Nixon's role in policymaking by saying, "If you give me a week, I'll think of something." Nixon's failed contest against Kennedy in 1960 suggested that his years of abrasive politics had undermined his appeal to voters who preferred someone more genial like Eisenhower. Although Kennedy was no Eisenhower, his youth and the suggestion of something fresh in his politics helped carry the day. Besides, Kennedy's false assertion that Eisenhower-Nixon had left us with a "missile gap" threatening the nation's security gave him an edge over Nixon that was vital in so closely contested an election.

Nixon could never accept defeat or concede that he was less than a great man deserving of the highest office. No sooner did he lose the 1960 presidential election than he began planning to make a comeback by running for the governorship of California in 1962. But again he fell short; this time against the incumbent governor, Edmund G. "Pat" Brown, a popular Democrat. Frustrated and angered by the statewide press that had generally opposed his candidacy and contributed to his defeat, Nixon held a press conference in which he famously scolded the assembled media, "Just think how much you're going to be missing. You won't have Nixon to kick around anymore, because, gentlemen, this is my last press conference," which of course it wasn't.

Between 1963 and 1968 Nixon worked tirelessly to prepare for another presidential campaign. He aimed to convince Americans and the press that he was above all an expert on foreign affairs—someone well prepared to manage the competition with the Soviet Union and China in the Cold War, and especially the growing war in Vietnam. During these five years, Nixon had honed his image as a foreign affairs expert by constant travel abroad—thirteen trips to Europe, Asia, the Middle East, and Africa—and an implicit promise that he would imitate Eisenhower's record on Korea by ending an unpopular war in Southeast Asia.

Vice President Hubert Humphrey, his opponent in the 1968 election, had the misfortune of being identified with LBJ and the conflict.

Yet despite Humphrey's handicap of being second-in-command during Johnson's turbulent four years, Nixon had to overcome his own track record of past defeats and political skullduggery. Henry Kissinger, who would become Nixon's national security adviser and secretary of state, said privately of Nixon in 1968, "That man is not fit to be president." Nixon's greatest fear during the campaign was that Johnson would reach a settlement in the war and remove the issue from the campaign. Johnson's March 31 speech withdrawing from a reelection fight and proposing peace talks with North Vietnam particularly worried Nixon. To counter Johnson's move toward a settlement, Nixon secretly sent word to the South Vietnamese government in Saigon that they would get a better peace deal from a Nixon administration than from a quick agreement arranged by Johnson. Although Johnson and Humphrey knew what Nixon was up to from wiretaps on conversations in Saigon's Washington embassy, Humphrey chose not to blow the whistle on Nixon's illegal interference in the peace talks. (Johnson called it an act of "treason.") It made a significant difference in a close election that Nixon won by a narrow popular margin—43.4 percent to Humphrey's 42.7 percent; Alabama's George Wallace received 13.5 percent of the vote running on a third-party ticket. Nixon, however, did win 301 electoral votes.

Nixon's greatest challenge as president was to end the Vietnam War and create what he and national security adviser Henry Kissinger called a structure of peace. But Nixon was not unmindful of domestic challenges to the economy and the environment. By 1970, the cost of the war had increased the federal deficit and burdened the country with inflation and a recession that threatened to defeat him in a 1972 reelection campaign. A new word entered into the language: "stagflation," rising unemployment with inflation. Remembering his time at the Office of Price Administration during World War II,

Nixon turned to wage and price controls while promoting more deficit spending to spur the economy and reduce unemployment. "We are all Keynesians now," Nixon declared. And though it temporarily improved the economy, it proved to be no more than a pause in the fight for economic control. As Nixon's biographer John Farrell points out, in 1973 and 1974, after the controls were removed, inflation increased to 10 to 12 percent while the stock market went into a two-year decline that cut its value in half. The rise of the OPEC oil-producing countries that increased fuel prices fourfold and compelled rationing at the pump undermined Nixon's reputation as a wise steward of the economy. Nixon was no slouch about meeting popular demand for political action regardless of his conservative antigovernment credentials. When an oil spill off the California coast polluted the waters near Santa Barbara, Nixon spoke out for environmental protection. At the beginning of 1970, he signed the National Environmental Policy Act that mandated studies of federal actions affecting the environment. In response to Earth Day that spring, Nixon established the Environmental Protection Agency (EPA) to preserve the country's natural resources and signed measures to protect the oceans and reduce pollution in the atmosphere, especially in Southern California, where automobile exhausts covered the area with a blanket of smog. Following in the footsteps of the two Roosevelts and Lyndon Johnson, Nixon won praise from organizations like Greenpeace and the Sierra Club for his environmental leadership.

While he certainly hoped his shift toward liberal domestic policies would resonate with most voters and later historians, his greatest investment was in transforming American foreign policy, especially in Vietnam and in relations with China and the Soviet Union, to reduce chances of a catastrophic nuclear conflict. Understanding that Americans were fed up with the war and the loss of so many lives in a futile struggle, he was determined to end the conflict. But he was also eager to find a way out of the constant tensions with communist adversaries, especially because Sino-Soviet differences opened the way to an initiative that could exploit their fears of each other. He was ready to abandon his long history of bashing "Red China," saying, "We do not want 800 million people living in angry isolation." He instructed Kissinger to begin secret conversations with Chinese representatives in Warsaw, Poland. As for the Middle East with its enduring antagonism between Israel and its Arab neighbors, he called it a "powder keg" that tempted great-power involvement threatening a wider war.

He was equally determined to achieve "peace with honor," which first meant ending the Vietnam War not with any agreement that looked like defeat, but as a settlement that gave South Vietnam the prospect of remaining independent from the North's communist regime. Understanding that Hanoi would not simply abandon its goal of unifying the peninsula, Nixon felt compelled to drive the North Vietnamese into a settlement by making the war so devastating, in excess of anything Johnson had done, that they would accept an arrangement that neither side would see as a humiliating defeat.

When Nixon insisted that there be mutual withdrawal of forces from South Vietnam and a POW exchange, Hanoi showed no interest in the proposal, demanding instead a departure of U.S. troops and an end to the existing pro-American government in Saigon. In March and April 1969, as a response to fresh attacks by the North Vietnamese, Nixon ordered the secret bombing of North Vietnamese bases in Cambodia. Because public knowledge of the air raids threatened to touch off new protests in the United States, Nixon wanted them hidden. But leaks about the raids triggered newspaper stories that enraged Nixon, who privately demanded action against leakers. Nixon now complained that the press was not only his but also the country's enemy. He was careful, however, to keep his complaints out of the public eye.

When Hanoi showed no inclination to soften its stance in the war, Nixon nonetheless described great success with "Vietnamization," meaning shifting responsibility of military combat to Saigon and the withdrawal of U.S. troops over time. He planned to bring home fifty thousand troops from Vietnam in 1969. Because he understood that having majority sentiment on his side was essential in advancing his foreign policy and winning reelection, he had no qualms about putting out misstatements and exaggerating the importance and success of what he did.

In the spring of 1970, with 84 percent of a poll favoring U.S. troop withdrawal from Vietnam, Nixon tried to satisfy public sentiment by recalling another hundred thousand troops from Vietnam and reducing draft calls. Because peace talks remained stalled and communist reinforcements on the Ho Chi Minh Trail through Cambodia were as great as ever, and a communist takeover of that country seemed imminent, Nixon was determined to counter the threat. Although he knew that an offensive seemed certain to generate renewed criticism, he would not back down. Besides, here was an opportunity to test the effectiveness of the South Vietnamese forces they had been training and supplying. Rallying public opinion, Nixon spoke to the nation to reassure it that we were not opening a new front in the war, but protecting our forces in South Vietnam. He described an apocalyptic moment when the United States could not act "like a pitiful, helpless giant." Otherwise, "the forces of totalitarianism and anarchy will threaten free nations and free institutions throughout the world." He ended with the declaration that "We will not be humiliated. We will not be defeated." His rhetoric was meant to convince people that he was a great president saving civilization from the barbarians.

The Cambodian "incursion" touched off an explosion of national protests, especially on college campuses, including Kent State in Ohio, where four students were killed by National Guard troops. It shook Nixon, who seemed to become unhinged—drinking to excess and privately cursing protesters and journalists attacking him. Kissinger did not escape the protests either. He had to move into the White House to avoid demonstrators around his apartment vilifying him with signs saying "Fuck Henry Kissinger" and accusing him of being a "war criminal."

Because the war in Vietnam remained stalemated and Hanoi would not agree to a peace arrangement that saved the United States from the stigma of defeat, Nixon agreed to yet another offensive that threatened to ignite fresh demonstrations but might pressure the North Vietnamese into more agreeable concessions. In 1971, it was an operation in Laos that relied on South Vietnamese forces. The attack turned into a disaster, with Saigon's troops fleeing the battlefield. Nixon put the best possible face on the defeat, saying that the battle was a success and had deterred the North from launching a fresh offensive against the South. He insisted to his aides that the attack had to be described as a "win." But in private he was scathing about the South Vietnamese. He said, "If the South Vietnamese could just win one cheap one . . . Take a stinking hill. . . . Bring back a prisoner or two. Anything." When South Vietnamese fighter planes failed to attack enemy trucks because they were "moving targets," Nixon shouted, "Bullshit. Just, just, just cream the fuckers!" He dismissed their excuse as "ridiculous."

He vented his anger on the press, which gave honest accounts of the fighting and the demonstration of Saigon's inability to combat the communist forces. He privately attacked the reporters and their editors as "against the war" and all too ready to report every setback in the fighting. He told Kissinger, "The news broadcasters are, of course, trying to kill us." The public saw through Nixon's attempts to put a false face on the results of the Laos campaign. Sixty-five percent of Americans did not accept administration accounts of the war. Commentators now described Nixon as creating the same credibility gap that had plagued Johnson. To combat the impression of a failing strategy in Vietnam, Nixon announced an increase in troop withdrawals by the end of the year as evidence that Vietnamization was working and that we would soon have peace with honor in Vietnam. But a majority of Americans no longer believed him.

With Nixon's efforts to end the war falling short, he turned to what he saw as the larger issue of how to rein in the Cold War, advance the cause of world peace and, not the least of his goals, assure his prospects for reelection. In addition, he believed that an upswing in relations with both China and Russia could win their support in helping him end the Vietnam War. In June 1971, the Chinese signaled their interest in having Kissinger come to Peking for preliminary discussions that could lead to a Nixon visit in 1972. Mindful that '72 was an election year in the United States, the Chinese sensed that Nixon would jump at the chance to excite public approval with a historic breakthrough in Sino-American relations. Kissinger's visit to China in July 1971 "laid the groundwork for you and Mao to turn a page in history . . . The process we have now started will send enormous shock waves around the world," Kissinger told Nixon. During his conversations in Peking, Kissinger emphasized American regard for China's standing as a great power and offered assurances that the United States would not collude with Moscow against them.

Nixon saw the opening to China as not only defusing tensions with Peking but also as a means of pressuring Moscow into concessions and improving his political standing as he began his reelection campaign. To make the strongest possible domestic impression, Nixon insisted on having the Chinese accept a ground station that could broadcast live TV pictures of his visit back to the United States.

In February 1972, Nixon preceded his weeklong stay in Peking with tutorials on what he could expect in his conversations with Mao Tse-tung, the architect of China's revolution, and Chou En-lai, his first lieutenant. France's André Malraux, de Gaulle's cultural affairs minister who knew both Chinese leaders, advised Nixon that they were indifferent to the outside world and thought only about China's self-interest. They were eager to arrange U.S. help in making China a great power. Kissinger, who had had two conversations with Chou on his preliminary visits to Peking, thought the Chinese wanted U.S. support in combating a Soviet threat, a resurgent Japan, and an independent Taiwan, where their Nationalist foes had taken refuge after losing control of the mainland. Because Nixon wanted to win exclusive credit for the transformation in relations, he insisted that he emerge alone from the plane after landing in Peking, the sole architect of this diplomatic revolution. At his first meeting with Mao, there was mutual stroking of egos: Nixon said that they needed to put past differences aside and accept that a nation's internal governing philosophy was of little importance alongside its relations with the world and especially us. Nixon and Mao agreed to leave political matters to their deputies and focus instead on "philosophic problems." The next six days were a well-choreographed ballet that, above all, made clear to Moscow that the U.S. and China were standing together against what the Chinese called "hegemonic aspirations" by the "normalization of relations."

When the meetings ended and the Nixon delegation headed home with a stop in Shanghai, the president became fearful that his trip would become the topic of criticism rather than praise in the United

States. Kissinger later described Nixon as "this lonely, tortured and insecure man," whose "success seemed to unsettle Nixon more than failure. He seemed obsessed by the fear that he was not receiving adequate credit." He particularly complained about the press, which he was sure would denounce what he had done as a betrayal of Taiwan. The trip in fact was hailed as a triumph of pragmatic leadership.

Following the trip, Nixon gave a press conference looking toward the 1972 elections, in which he took pains to advance comity and consensus, emphasizing his eagerness for peace in Vietnam and better relations with both Russia and China. It was a sharp contrast with his private recorded discussions, but it demonstrated a keen political sense of what the country wanted to hear.

Guided by Kissinger, Nixon turned their successful rapprochement with China into a weapon for pressuring Moscow into agreements with the United States described as détente. In October 1971, Anatoly Dobrynin, the Soviet ambassador in Washington, complained to Kissinger about the poor state of Soviet-American relations, saying they were in the worst condition since the Cuban missile crisis in 1962. Kissinger agreed and said that Nixon was eager to remedy this by moving forward on arms control—Strategic Arms Limitation Talks (SALT)—and a summit meeting. Anxious about advances in Sino-American relations, Moscow announced its readiness to sign a SALT treaty and hold a summit meeting in Moscow in the spring of 1972, after Nixon had been to Peking. Nixon's initiative with Moscow did not sit well with conservatives in the United States who were troubled by reductions in ICBMs. The administration fended off their criticism with assurances that the development of antiballistic missiles (ABMs) gave the United States new security against a Soviet surprise attack.

Conservative doubts did not deter Nixon from working for better relations with Moscow that he saw as essential to international peace. In April 1972, he sent Kissinger to Moscow to arrange a summit conference with Soviet leader Leonid Brezhnev in May. The sixty-six-year-old Ukraine-born Brezhnev had presided over the Soviet Union since 1964 and been instrumental in its acquisition of modern armaments that made it a formidable military rival of the United States. An eagerness to raise his country's living standards led Brezhnev to cooperate with the United States in trade and arms control as well as in deterring Washington from allying itself with Peking against the Soviet Union. Kissinger went to Moscow with instructions to emphasize Nixon's interest in Soviet help to end the Vietnam War. Although the Soviets honestly explained that they did not control North Vietnam, Nixon and Brezhnev nevertheless remained attracted enough by the possibilities of a summit that they agreed to meet in May.

The weeklong summit beginning on May 22 was an exercise in mutual maneuvering for advantage. Because Nixon's delegation assumed that listening devices were monitoring all of their conversations, Nixon held some private discussions in his limousine parked in the courtyard of his residence. In their first meeting, Nixon and Brezhnev were cordial to each other, demonstrating the need each felt to make their meetings productive of agreements they could advertise to their domestic audiences. Brezhnev evoked memories of World War II U.S.-Soviet cooperation as a model for them to emulate. They ended their first meeting by agreeing that they must not succumb to a military conflict provoked by some other adversaries, acknowledging that neither of them would be drawn into a conflict by China. In a more formal meeting the next day, they largely agreed on a SALT treaty that would leave each side with enough arms to destroy each other while reducing the costs of an arms race. An interest in increased trade dominated subsequent talks, though reaching any agreement here meant addressing a variety of technical matters that were left to a commission holding future talks on lend-lease debt, bank credits, trade, and most favored nation details.

On Vietnam and tangled relations in the Middle East, where the United States was aligned with Israel and the Soviets with the Arab states, the bars to agreement were too high to surmount. Yet Kissinger had made clear to Brezhnev that if the North Vietnamese would agree to a peace settlement, in time, they could resume their fight to conquer the South without renewed U.S. interference. The conference ended with pronouncements on the arms control agreement and future plans for economic exchange that could advance the prosperity of both nations. Like FDR on his return from Yalta in 1945, Nixon addressed a joint congressional session, declaring, "New hopes are rising for a world no longer shadowed by fear and want and war." Forty-eight years later, there was a realistic basis to Nixon's pronouncement about a peaceful Soviet-American future, tough without a hint that it would be without a Soviet regime.

Vietnam, however, remained a continuing dilemma. Although Nixon cut call-ups with a plan to end the draft entirely by January 1973, thousands of American troops continued to die in the fighting, and the North Vietnamese remained determined to win control of the South. Peace talks in Paris ground on with no end in sight until September 1972, when the North Vietnamese agreed to make peace. Kissinger found dealing with both Vietnamese sides maddening. Privately, he said, "The Vietnamese, North and South, are really maniacs. . . . You never can be sure that one of them won't do something suicidal. They're both insane." Persuaded by a U.S. commitment not to insist on a North Vietnamese withdrawal of troops from the South and a willingness for Hanoi to have a say in Saigon's political future, which was animated by Nixon's eagerness to get a preliminary settlement before the November election, both sides announced their readiness to conclude the war. Kissinger famously declared, "Peace is at hand." But reporters wanted to know what there was about the settlement that could not have been achieved in 1969. Neither Nixon nor Kissinger had a persuasive answer.

Because final details remained to be worked out, Nixon worried that Hanoi might renege on the preliminary agreement before the election on November 7. They did not, and Nixon defeated Senator George McGovern in a landslide, winning forty-nine of fifty states and 60.7 percent of the popular vote, the third greatest in presidential history. Nixon told Kissinger that if Hanoi wouldn't cooperate with them after November 7, "we'll bomb the bastards." The loss of both congressional houses to the Democrats tainted Nixon's victory. He expected Republicans to blame him and told his aide H. R. Haldeman, "Make sure that we start pissing on the party before they begin pissing on me. Blame bad candidates and poor organization."

But the bigger postelection challenge was to close out the war. Nixon believed that he had to end the fighting before the start of his second term lest it distract from his larger designs. But ending the war proved to be more difficult than Nixon and Kissinger expected. Saigon resisted signing an agreement that left Hanoi's forces in the South, where they could launch another offensive. Assurances that Nixon would come to their aid if this occurred did not convince Saigon. Similarly, the North Vietnamese would not agree to alter anything they had agreed to.

The stalemate convinced Nixon that he had to resume the bombing of the North despite a poll in which 52 percent of Americans favored a withdrawal and clean break with South Vietnam. But Nixon assumed that if no American troops were being killed and no young men were being drafted, most Americans wouldn't object to a new bombing campaign. The failure to get a settlement angered Kissinger, who described all the Vietnamese as "just a bunch of shits." Meeting both sides in the Vietnamese negotiations, he said, was tantamount to running "an insane asylum." On December 18, Nixon launched the bombing campaign. It consisted of around-the-clock attacks that struck Hanoi and Haiphong, the North's principal harbor. The United States lost fifteen B-52s in the raids, fourteen more than had been previously shot down. The devastation from the bombing was so great that it forced Hanoi back to the peace table in January. The threat of more bombing, and unrelenting pressure on South Vietnam to sign a peace agreement, finally brought the war to an end. Hanoi saw it as an opportunity to recoup its losses and prepare for a future assault on the South without U.S. interference, and Saigon complained privately of a "sellout."

Although Nixon and Kissinger knew full well that Hanoi would eventually move successfully to conquer the South, Nixon described the settlement to the country as "peace with honor." Kissinger publicly expressed hope that the peace could hold, but privately he said, "If they're lucky [meaning the South Vietnamese], they can hold out for a year or two." Kissinger had it right; the North Vietnamese took over the South in 1975.

Vietnam wasn't Nixon's only frustration. The Middle East, where Israel and the Arab states continued to threaten each other, posed a constant jeopardy to peace, not only in the region but to Washington and Moscow: The United States had political and moral ties to Tel Aviv as the region's only democracy, and the Soviets had aligned themselves with Egypt and the Arabs more generally. A 1967 six-day war between the two sides in the Middle East had inflicted an embarrassing defeat on Egypt, Jordan, and Syria: The Israelis seized the Gaza Strip and the Sinai Peninsula from Egypt, the West Bank of the

Jordan River and East Jerusalem from Jordan, and the Golan Heights from Syria. The USSR, as the Arabs' protector, had also suffered a humiliating setback. The same year, the Israelis became a nuclear power with the construction of two atomic bombs. It raised the possibility of a nuclear disaster in a future conflict.

By 1973, with Soviet help, the Arab states had rebuilt their militaries and launched a surprise attack on Israel in what became known as the Yom Kippur War, which lasted nineteen days in October. Egypt and Syria scored some initial victories, but the Israelis quickly recouped their losses and inflicted new defeats on them. When the Israelis surrounded the Egyptian Third Army in the Sinai, it opened a Soviet-American crisis. The Soviets proposed to Washington that they agree to a joint enterprise to rescue the Egyptian army from disaster. But the Nixon administration refused and raised the DEFCON, or defense condition, to a level not seen since the 1962 Cuban missile crisis. The danger of a Soviet-American confrontation passed when Moscow backed away from sending paratroops to the Sinai.

When a truce was agreed to on October 25, there remained the challenge of separating the two armies from one another. Because the Egyptians and Israelis would not talk to each other, Kissinger took the initiative of mediating. In January 1974, he began a round of shuttle diplomacy, flying between Israel and Egypt. Kissinger's role as an intermediary in the discussions was crucial in establishing a more stable peace. Between February 25 and March 4, Kissinger shuttled between Tel Aviv and Damascus to arrange the separation of Israeli and Syrian troops. For four weeks in April and May he shuttled continually between all the Middle East capitals, including Riyadh, Saudi Arabia, and Amman, Jordan, to advance Middle East peace and bring an end to an oil embargo that forced rationing of fuel in the United States. The Nixon-Kissinger initiative opened the way to Egyptian-Israeli talks that would come to fruition four years later under President Jimmy Carter.

The Nixon-Kissinger advances in the Middle East were not replicated in Latin America. Preoccupied with preventing increased Soviet-Cuban influence in the Western Hemisphere, the Nixon administration continued the stalemate in relations with Fidel Castro's pro-Soviet Cuban government. More important, Nixon and Kissinger were greatly troubled by developments in Chile. In 1970, after the election of Salvador Allende, an avowed Marxist and leader of his country's Socialist Party, Nixon and Kissinger feared he might represent a threat to U.S. interests across the hemisphere. They shared a subordinate official's belief that Latin America was "a priority target for enemies of the U.S. We must ensure that it is neither turned against us nor taken over by those who threaten our vital national interests." Although Kissinger had dismissed the southern republics as "a dagger pointed at the heart of Antarctica," he and Nixon saw Allende as a menace. Kissinger told Nixon that his election "poses for us one of the most serious challenges ever faced in this hemisphere." Kissinger also told the president that communists and "extreme Socialists" were in control of the Chilean government and that they had cowed opposition voices into submission. He added to Nixon's sense of urgency when Allende recognized Castro's Cuban government and the Organization of American States (OAS) refused to oppose Allende's regime.

Despite Allende's general popularity in Chile and across Latin America, Nixon and Kissinger were eager to oust him. They saw ties to Chile's military leaders, press stories about subversion in Chile of the democratic process abetted by Moscow, and economic measures as the best way to depose him. By the beginning of 1972, U.S. economic pressure had joined with Allende's nationalizing of foreign-owned companies and labor walkouts to produce 20 percent inflation and food shortages, undermining Allende's popularity. While Washington was more eager than ever to topple Allende and the CIA gave $6 million to Allende's domestic opponents, it was equally determined to hide its part in any upheaval. In September 1973, when the Chilean military overthrew Allende and assassinated him, the CIA director told Kissinger that "while the Agency was instrumental in enabling opposition political parties and media to . . . maintain their dynamic resistance to the Allende regime, the CIA played no direct role in the events which led to the establishment of the new military government." Nixon and Kissinger denied any advance knowledge of the coup, which was untrue. While they privately agreed that they had not arranged the coup, they acknowledged that they had "helped them—created the conditions as much as possible." Kissinger wanted the State Department to say, "We do not support revolutions as a means of settling disputes," which subsequent actions supporting the successor Pinochet regime demonstrated was false.

While Nixon and Kissinger took satisfaction from helping to overthrow a left-wing government in Latin America, domestic and international politics dictated that they hide their sense of accomplishment.

By contrast, Nixon had considerable frustration over his attempts to put conservatives on the Supreme Court. In 1969 and 1970, Nixon had first nominated federal judge Clement Haynsworth of South Carolina and then Judge G. Harrold Carswell of Georgia to fill a vacancy on the court. Both nominees were seen as temperamentally unfit and failed to win Senate majorities. True, Democratic Party control of the Senate made a difference. But despite opposing party control, Nixon won approval for subsequent nominees Harry Blackmun of Minnesota, Lewis Powell of Virginia, and William Rehnquist of Arizona, all of whom were seen as eminently qualified to serve on the high court.

Whatever Nixon's achievements and missteps, his administration remains most notable for the Watergate scandal that brought him down.[1] The problem began with what Nixon called a third-rate burglary. But because it involved the Committee to Reelect the President (CREEP), it raised questions about Nixon's involvement: "What did the President know and if so, when did he know it?" Nixon always denied any role in ordering the break-in at the Democratic Party headquarters, but the pursuit of the truth by Judge John Sirica, *Washington Post* reporters Bob Woodward and Carl Bernstein, and a Senate investigating committee headed by North Carolina Democrat Sam Ervin intensified the view that this was a scandal that led directly to the White House. More specifically, the issue became not whether Nixon had initiated the break-in to gather damaging evidence on McGovern and the Democrats, but whether the president was involved in a cover-up effort to shield members of his administration who were involved. As John Dean, Nixon's White House counsel who turned against him, put it, "Nixon thought I should lie for him. I should fall on the sword. . . . I should go to jail indefinitely so he can continue to be who he wants to be. I didn't see it that way."

While no one ever demonstrated that Nixon ordered the break-in, there was ample evidence that he set a tone that facilitated the crime. His deviousness and inclination to cut corners, regardless of the fact that any extralegal steps were entirely unnecessary in the 1972 election, formed the backdrop to his fall from power. More important, it was not the break-in that brought Nixon down, but the cover-up which he led. His demise rested on the decision of White House aides, led by John Dean, to limit their exposure to criminal charges by telling the truth about Nixon's actions.

To save himself, in the spring of 1974, Nixon dismissed H. R. Haldeman and John Ehrlichman, his two principal aides. At the same time, Nixon aimed to reorganize the FBI and CIA, both of which he believed a threat to him. He saw them as staffed with "Ivy League" and "Georgetown set" personnel who held him in contempt.

Nixon also had to deal with a combative congressional opposition. Pressed by the Senate Judiciary Committee, Attorney General Elliot Richardson appointed a Watergate special prosecutor, Harvard law professor and former solicitor general Archibald Cox. In July 1973, when White House aide Alexander Butterfield told the Ervin Committee about a voice-activated White House taping system, Cox and Nixon began a legal struggle over access to the tapes. Never mind that Kennedy and Johnson had taped telephone and face-to-face White House conversations that remained closed. (Most of them are now open.) It was Nixon's secret tapes that could reveal whether the president had been involved in a cover-up of wrongdoing. Advised to destroy the tapes, Nixon refused—convinced that executive privilege would allow him to resist any access to tapes of conversations he had made.

Nixon was determined to protect himself from Cox's aggressive inquiry by firing Cox. When Richardson, the attorney general and his second-in-command, resigned rather than follow Nixon's orders, Robert Bork, the solicitor general, complied in what became known as the Saturday Night Massacre. Nixon then abolished the office of special prosecutor, intensifying charges against him of covering up crimes and forcing him to retreat and appoint Leon Jaworski, a distinguished Texas attorney, as a new special prosecutor. Jaworski pressed the case for access to Nixon's tapes and won a decision from the Supreme Court, saying that possible prosecution of criminal behavior exceeded any claim of executive privilege.

In August 1974, when a June 23, 1972, tape became public, it made clear that Nixon had orchestrated a Watergate cover-up. It was called the "smoking gun" tape and assured that Nixon would become the second president in American history to be impeached. People in his inner circle worried that in response he might commit suicide or try to order a military coup. Happily for the country, he accepted the likely verdict of Congress—impeachment and conviction in a Senate trial that would force him from office. So instead of waiting for congressional action, he decided to become the first U.S. president to resign from office. In a final speech he gave to the nation, he ended with words that others might want to take to heart: "Always remember, others may hate you—but those who hate you don't win unless you hate them, and then you destroy yourself."

The Watergate scandal has eclipsed Nixon's impressive achievements in foreign affairs. Moreover, it has shaped future thinking by presidents about how far they can go in defying traditional democratic norms. However much they might like to ignore Congress and run roughshod over opponents, they operate in the shadow of Watergate and Nixon's resignation. Still, they appreciate that if their party controls one congressional house, they are unlikely to be forced from office. It is enough to encourage defiance of the House of Representatives. The impeachment of Bill Clinton for lying about his relations with Monica Lewinsky that led to his vindication in the Senate, or at least nonconviction, was a powerful check on future Congresses that might otherwise have been ready to impeach a president. As important, it persuaded some presidents that they could be more imperious than otherwise. The struggle between a president and an opposition House is as alive today as when the Constitution put the system of checks and balances in place.

CHAPTER 9

Jimmy Carter

The Moralist as Politician

===

Richard Nixon's resignation threw a cloud over the Republican Party that dogged his successor Gerald Ford. Although Ford's pronouncement that our long national nightmare was over suggested that he would distance himself from Nixon in the twenty-nine months remaining in his second term, Ford's decision to pardon Nixon in hope of putting a decisive end to the Watergate scandal unfairly tarred him with complicity in wrongdoing.

In 1976, when Ford tried to win the presidency in his own right, he came up against Jimmy Carter, the fifty-one-year-old, one-term Democratic governor of Georgia. As an outsider—no Georgian had ever been elected to the White House; and southerners, 110 years after the Civil War, were still identified with rebellion against the Union—Carter was a long shot to win the election. But voter alienation toward Ford over the Nixon pardon gave Carter a thirty-point popular advantage at the start of the campaign. Still, Carter was no world-beater as a national politician. His performance in three televised debates with Ford raised more questions than they settled about Carter's preparation to be president. But Ford's fared even worse: After more than two years as president, he came across as amazingly ignorant about foreign affairs. He stumbled badly when he declared that the Soviet Union did not dominate Eastern Europe. One reporter said: That was Jerry just talking about something he knew nothing about. Later in the campaign, Carter undercut himself as well when he told a reporter for *Playboy* magazine that he had lusted toward women and committed adultery "in his heart," remarks that were widely mocked. The campaign seemed to have become a contest between two unskilled candidates doing more to lose than win a presidential election. In the end, Carter eked out a victory—propelled by a national hunger for change and a stagnant economy with 7.7 percent unemployment.

Jimmy Carter came to the presidency from an admirable background of public service as a graduate of the Naval Academy, duty on nuclear submarines, a two-term Georgia state senator, and governor of Georgia from 1971 to 1975. During his governorship, he had established himself as a devoted advocate of equal rights for African Americans—not a popular position to take in 1970s Georgia. As Stuart Eizenstat, a principal Carter aide on domestic affairs, pointed out in a biography, Carter was a southern populist whose grandfather had been a close associate of the earlier Georgia populist Tom Watson. Carter identified himself with ordinary Americans who struggled to make a living and lead moral lives. His public pledges "I will never lie to you" and "a government as good as its people" were compelling slogans in a post-Vietnam and -Watergate era.

In 1974, as Carter's gubernatorial term was coming to an end, he saw Nixon's demise as an unprecedented chance for a populist Democrat to win the White House. As president, Eizenstat asserts, Carter lacked many of the principal attributes of most twentieth-century presidents. "But," Eizenstat adds, Carter "brought to the Oval Office his own unique intellect, inquisitiveness, self-discipline, political courage, and resilience in the face of setbacks." Most of all, he is now recalled for his morality—his unyielding commitment to Christian principles of honesty and humane treatment of peoples everywhere, as well as a profound abhorrence of the prospect of nuclear war.

On taking office in January 1977, Carter confronted challenges at home and abroad that tested all his abilities and resilience. From the start, he intended to separate himself and his administration from the corruption and secretiveness that were then the most memorable features of Nixon's administration.

During Carter's limo ride to the White House from the inauguration, he exited the car and walked hand in hand with his wife, Rosalynn, for a mile on Pennsylvania Avenue—symbolizing a new openness in government. And to rid the country of the enduring recrimination over Vietnam, he pardoned those who had burned their draft cards or fled to Canada to escape service in the war and faced indictments for draft dodging.[1]

Carter began his presidency with recollections of Harry Truman and the similarity of the problems that bedeviled him and still confronted Carter, especially in foreign affairs: peace, human rights, arms control, and the Middle East. Keeping the peace in the face of Soviet and Chinese "adventurism" and advancing the cause of human rights everywhere were noble but elusive ambitions. Carter inherited the terrifying prospect of having to fight a nuclear war, and he knew that his predecessors had been tempted to use these weapons in Korea and Vietnam as well as during the Cuban missile crisis. Truman and Eisenhower had rejected suggestions of using atomic bombs against China during the Korean fighting; Kennedy had turned aside actions against Soviet arms in Cuba that could have triggered a nuclear exchange; and Johnson had resisted proposals to defeat or at least intimidate the North Vietnamese with the threat of a nuclear attack. If aides had followed through on everything Nixon said in his private ravings, we could have triggered a nuclear war. Carter understood, as the diplomat and historian George Kennan had believed, that no human being is to be trusted with control of these weapons of mass destruction.[2]

Yet Carter's eagerness to reduce the threat of a nuclear holocaust could not always be reconciled with the pressure to deter Soviet aggression. He promised in his inaugural speech the "elimination of all nuclear weapons from this earth." In 1979, however, in response to Soviet deployment of SS-20 mobile missiles across Eastern Europe that could destroy Western Europe's principal cities, Carter ordered the deployment of U.S. Pershing and cruise missiles. When I went to Belgrade and then Moscow in 1979, on the fortieth anniversary of the outbreak of World War II under a State Department cultural exchange program, I met with three Soviet historians attached to the Center for the Study of the United States and Canada. They refused to believe that I was an independent scholar. They lobbied me about the Pershing and cruise missiles, which I knew nothing more about than what I had read in the newspapers. It was an unforgettable personal moment in the larger Cold War. In 1999, when I returned to Russia—this time for the Franklin and Eleanor Roosevelt Institute in Hyde Park, New York—and spoke to graduate students, they remained convinced that the military controlled the United States and were intent on undermining their country.

Soviet agitation over the U.S. deployments in 1979 led them to increase tensions with Washington by putting a brigade in Cuba and invading Afghanistan to bolster a communist regime. Carter also saw Moscow as posing a threat to the Persian Gulf and Western oil supplies. The Soviet invasion solidified anti-Russian feeling in the U.S. Senate, which had been simmering in response to Soviet involvement in African civil wars, and which blocked the ratification of a strategic arms limitation treaty Carter had signed with Brezhnev in June 1979.

Carter's frustration at the downturn in Soviet relations extended to Iran as well. As a staunch advocate of human rights, Carter had felt compelled to raise the issue of human rights abuses in Iran by the shah's secret police, SAVAK, during the shah's visit to the White House in November 1977. Carter considered the shah a "strong ally" but feared that he was losing control of his country because of his regime's repression. In his conversation with Carter, the shah refused to give any ground, saying that he was combating communist subversion. On a reciprocal visit to Tehran in December, Carter quoted an ancient Persian poet to the shah: "If the misery of others leave you indifferent and with no feeling of sorrow, then you cannot be called a human being." Carter was making clear that American values were at odds with the shah's repression.

Unresponsive to Carter's warnings, the shah declared martial law in December 1978. By January 1979, it was clear that Iran's popular religious leader, the seventy-six-year-old Ayatollah Khomeini, who was exiled in Paris, commanded widespread support to replace the shah as the head of state. His sermons denouncing the shah and the United States were recorded on cassettes and distributed to mosques in Iran, reaching millions of people. Despite the shah's slow demise, Carter felt compelled to continue to support him as a reliable ally. In response, Khomeini attacked America as the "great Satan." In February, when the shah left his country initially to find sanctuary in Morocco, the ayatollah flew to Tehran, where he received a hero's welcome. In October, when the shah became ill with malignant lymphoma, Carter agreed to let him come to New York for medical treatment. The U.S. embassy in Tehran informed the Iranian government that this was strictly a humanitarian action without political implications.

Such assurances initially prompted the Iranian government to promise to protect the embassy if it came under attack, but it could not or did not choose to control some three thousand Iranian militants, who on November 4 overran the U.S. embassy and took sixty-six American hostages. Memories of the CIA's role in overturning the government of Mohammad Mossadegh in 1953 fanned suspicions of another U.S. plot to restore the shah to power. Carter had anticipated such a reaction, asking his advisers, "What are you guys going to advise me to do when [the militants] overrun our embassy and take our people hostage?" No one had an answer. When the students who seized the embassy were lionized in Iran as revolutionary heroes, Khomeini sang their praises, joining in a call for the return of the shah to Iran for trial, and an ongoing crisis ensued. By April, when Khomeini's government still resisted releasing the hostages, Carter broke diplomatic relations. The Iranians released fourteen black and female hostages weeks after the takeover, but fifty-two remained in custody. Six other Americans, who were away from the embassy on other business in Tehran when their colleagues were captured, managed to escape Iran with the help of the Canadian embassy, which gave them cover as Canadian citizens. It sparked hope that the other Americans held in the embassy and the foreign ministry would see an end to their ordeal soon. (The Canadian operation was celebrated in a 2012 film, *Argo*.)

The ongoing crisis came on top of what had become known as the "malaise speech" in the summer of 1979. Carter had already been losing touch with national sentiment when he considered using "New

Foundations" as an identifying theme for the administration. But it never caught on, and fell short again when Barack Obama tried to revive the phrase a generation later. At an Obama White House dinner for presidential historians, Doris Kearns Goodwin observed it lacked the resonance of the New Deal, the New Frontier, or the Great Society. It sounded, Doris joked to me, like an ad for a woman's girdle.

The speech arose due to the latest swirl of bad economic developments: an oil embargo causing fuel shortages, long lines at gas stations, and inflation in the United States running at more than 11 percent a year. Pointing to the Organization of Petroleum Exporting Countries (OPEC), chiefly from the Middle East, as the villain did little to shift the blame away from the Carter White House. In July 1979, Carter's approval rating had fallen to a dismal 26 to 30 percent.

Carter tried to rally the country by giving a nationally televised energy speech. Instead, the speech further undermined his hold on the public. In an ill-advised attempt to deliver harsh truths, Carter described a "crisis of confidence" in the country brought on by self-indulgence and a loss of commitment to "hard work, strong families, close-knit communities and our faith in God." But Carter's dose of pessimism about the country's future ill served the national resolve to find solutions to its energy and economic troubles. Where former presidents like FDR drew the country together by emphasizing the nation's strengths in the midst of an unprecedented economic crisis, Carter emphasized the weaknesses that had taken over the national outlook. The public is addicted to optimism or what has been called "the power of positive thinking," not talk of malaise or debilitating difficulties. Where citizens saw FDR as the man who had overcome personal loss with his disability, Carter now seemed to be a scold, chiding the country for not reverting to earlier habits of stiff upper lip and determination to meet its malaise head on. When Carter next moved to fire members of his administration and reshuffle the government, it came across as doing more to dismantle than build a new successful structure.

Iran continued to hold the hostages for over a year despite diplomatic efforts by Carter and others to free them, making his administration—and America—look weak or unable to face down a radical Muslim country. Compounding Carter's problem were daily media stories recording the number of days the hostages had been held and the administration's failure to bring them home. Washington's unwillingness to trade the shah for the hostages, which the ayatollah was demanding, created an unbridgeable impasse in the discussions despite sending him out of the United States to Panama and then Egypt. An unwillingness to apply economic sanctions by mining waters around Iran that would cut off its oil exports and undermine its economy rested on a fear that the Iranians might then kill the hostages. The crisis amounted to a national humiliation, which called into question the country's military power and its resolve to support allies. In Eizenstat's words, "the hostages became a political albatross he [Carter] could not shake from his shoulders." With the example of an Israeli rescue mission in July 1976 of 102 hostages from Entebbe, Uganda, where they had been taken from a hijacked Air France plane flying from Paris to Tel Aviv, Carter turned to the U.S. military for a solution to the hostage crisis.

In the summer of 1980, in the midst of the hostage predicament, I attended a conference in London on World War II. I had no idea that William Casey, who had a keen interest in the war's studies and was a supporter of former California governor Ronald Reagan and the chairman of his emerging Republican campaign for president against Carter, had funded our travel. He attended our conference and I had breakfast with him one morning at the British army medical mess or dormitory, where we were housed. Little did I know that his presence at the conference was a possible cover for him to go on to Madrid, Spain, where he allegedly met with Iranians to arrange release of the hostages in return for an arms deal and an unfreezing of $12 billion in American-held Iranian funds. In 1987, when the House Intelligence Committee conducted an investigation into whether the Reagan campaign had broken any laws in 1980 in these secret negotiations, and into Casey's whereabouts that summer, I told a committee counsel member that I had seen him in London at our conference in July, and sent the counsel the records I had of the timing and conference agenda. When I agreed to testify before the committee, they asked if Casey had said anything over breakfast about travel to Madrid. All I could tell them was that I didn't see Casey for a few days at our conference sessions. My testimony may have encouraged assumptions that he had been away in Madrid negotiating with the Iranians, though neither the House committee nor a Senate committee found credible evidence that Casey had gone to Madrid or negotiated such a deal.[3]

By April 1980, diplomatic efforts to free the hostages had come to naught despite repeated initiatives. The best the White House could hope for was that the sitting of a new Iranian parliament might free the hostages in another five or six months. But Carter's patience had run out. He ordered his military to put a rescue plan in motion. Secretary of State Cyrus Vance, who all along had opposed any military steps of any kind as likely to fail and trigger the killing of some, if not all, of the hostages, refused to support the mission. In response, he gave Carter a letter of resignation, which Carter accepted.

However well planned, the mission on April 24 proved to be a disaster: Two helicopters were disabled in a sandstorm and the mission was aborted. One helicopter crashed into a C-130 transport plane; eight Americans were killed, and three injured and subsequently hospitalized. Carter was deeply affected by the men's bravery and the loss of lives. It was also a political disaster, and many sensed this meant the end of the Carter presidency.

It was not the last time Iran was to dog American politics. In 2015, Barack Obama concluded an agreement with the Iranians stipulating a suspension of their development of nuclear weapons for fifteen years in return for the end of U.S. economic sanctions that had cost Tehran $160 billion. The agreement included the unfreezing of Iranian funds in the United States, which Republicans denounced as a giveaway to Iran. America's European allies joined in the agreement. The Israelis had taken covert actions to deter the Iranians from acquiring nuclear weapons, and did not believe that the Iranians would honor the agreement or would discontinue their efforts to become a nuclear power. But the Europeans disagreed: They were convinced that the provisions of the agreement, which provided for "extraordinary and robust monitoring, verification, and inspection," would guard against cheating, which it did. It was only with Trump's repudiation of the agreement and the killing of Iran's top general that Iran abandoned that agreement.

The Carter hostage mission disaster joined with domestic economic problems—led by inflation—to increase the speculation that Carter could not be reelected in November 1980. But Carter was determined to run again in 1980. And though he had little prospect of improving the economy before the election or freeing the hostages, he could point to four major advances in foreign affairs: an international fight for human rights, including the reduction of nuclear threats to humankind; treaties with Panama about the canal; the Camp David accords Carter mediated between Egypt and Israel; and the reestablishment of relations with mainland China and new arrangements with the Nationalists on Taiwan.

In May 1977, Carter told an audience at the University of Notre Dame that he was committed to "a policy based on constant decency in its values and optimism in our historical vision." Carter was appealing to the country's better angels. He explained in his memoirs that his sense of injustice about racism in Georgia, across the South, and more generally in the whole nation schooled him in the need for respectful attitudes toward all human beings, or the application of "moral principles" at home and abroad. He was mindful of the argument about the contest in foreign policy between realism and idealism. He rejected the contention that realism should always eclipse idealism, and meaning that we cozy up to dictators as long as they sided with us against the Soviet Union. Carter believed that speaking out for human rights was a central part of the American tradition, going back to Thomas Jefferson and Woodrow Wilson, and should once again be at the center of our foreign policy. He was building on FDR's 1944 "Second Bill of Rights" speech, calling on the nation to give every American a subsistence income, assuring them of a decent life.

Carter pressed his case for human rights, especially with Soviet leaders who resented his interference, as they called it, in their internal affairs. Carter wrote later, "It will always be impossible to measure how much was accomplished by our nation's policy when the units of measurement are not inches or pounds or dollars. The lifting of the human spirit . . . the newfound sense of human dignity—these are difficult to quantify, but I am certain that many people were able to experience them because the United States of America let it be known that we stood for freedom and justice for all people."

In negotiating treaties with Panama for the transfer of the canal to that country, through whose territory it ran since its opening in 1914, Carter was mindful of America's reputation as a bully telling the southern republics how to govern themselves, and of complaints from left-wing political leaders across Latin America that the United States was nothing more than an old-style imperial nation dominating what it saw as its sphere of influence. But Carter was also aware of sentiment in the United States that we had built, paid for, and protected the canal for three quarters of a century, and owned it. In his 1976 campaign against Ford, Carter had pledged to hold on to the canal for "the foreseeable future."

After Carter entered the White House, he felt compelled to respond to pressure from seven Latin American countries to renegotiate the 1903 treaty that had given the United States perpetual control over the canal and required the U.S. to pay Panama $10 million and an annual $250,000 fee. Resentment against U.S. control was an enduring element of Panamanian politics, and by the 1960s had manifested in acts of violence that cost both American and Panamanian lives. After a 1964 riot, Lyndon Johnson had agreed to negotiate a new agreement for administering the canal. But negotiations under Johnson, Nixon, and Ford faced too much opposition in both capitals to reach a settlement.

Mindful of the security issue surrounding Soviet influence in Latin America, especially through Castro's Cuba, and the moral case the Panamanians had to control everything in their own land, Carter decided, despite powerful opposition in the United States to any diminished role in controlling the canal, to negotiate with the Panamanian government. Because forty-eight of the Senate's one hundred members signed a resolution against "giving away the Canal," signaling that Carter would not get two-thirds of the upper house to approve a treaty, his path to a successful negotiation looked bleak.

The negotiations, first with the Panamanians and then with U.S. senators, were difficult. The Panamanians did not want to perpetuate the U.S. right to defend the canal, which they saw as a breach of their sovereignty. Carter's chief negotiator, Sol Linowitz, took the initiative to propose that they negotiate two treaties: one about security and a second about administration. In the security agreement, the U.S. was granted the right to protect the canal from external threats, and the Panamanians would have responsibility for countering any internal threat to its safety. A second treaty agreed to transfer control of the canal at the end of 1999 to Panama. The treaties were formalized in a signing ceremony at the White House in September 1977, less than a year after Carter had been elected. It was reminiscent of Franklin Roosevelt's transition from gunboat diplomacy to his Good Neighbor policy, and a contrast with recent abusive rhetoric toward Mexican and Central American migrants trying to enter the United States.

Having overcome Panamanian resistance to any U.S. involvement in the canal's security, Carter had to convince sixty-seven senators to endorse his treaties, nothing his three immediate predecessors believed they could do. A twenty-two-day Senate debate and unrelenting White House pressure ultimately gave Carter the sixty-seven Senate votes he needed for confirmation. It was a victory for better U.S. relations across Latin America and for an administration struggling to prove its entitlement to a second term, but it also gave conservative Republicans a point of attack against Carter and the Democrats that they used to good effect in the 1980 presidential campaign.

An even greater accomplishment seemed possible if the administration could move Israel and the Arab states toward a more peaceful future. Progress in that direction had escaped every administration since the founding of Israel in 1948. Carter, who had visited Israel as governor of Georgia in 1973 and had a well-schooled knowledge of the Middle East through his earlier Bible studies, was eager to make regional peace a crowning achievement of his White House foreign policy. He also understood that "if our efforts failed, we would create an image of fumbling incompetence." He knew that "serious obstacles" stood in the way of anything resembling "a comprehensive peace settlement." He sympathized as well with the plight of the Palestinians, who had become a displaced people without a homeland in which they could live and prosper. He was determined to respond to the sense of hopelessness about peace and to depart from the hands-off approach of Presidents Eisenhower, Kennedy, Johnson, and Ford. But the Nixon-Kissinger initiatives in separating Arab and Israeli armies from each other after the 1973 war had given Carter a spark of hope that Washington could have an impact on the unrelenting tensions in the region.

Carter's initial meeting with Yitzhak Rabin, Israel's prime minister, in March 1977 did not go well, with Rabin unyielding on all of Carter's suggestions for compromise. Growing confidence in Israel's ability to defend itself, spawned by its victory in the 1967 war and its ultimate success in 1973, convinced Tel Aviv that it could withstand Arab aggression without significant concessions. In addition, Carter's refusal to pledge to move the U.S. embassy from Tel Aviv to Jerusalem, insisting that the status of the Holy City be settled in an Arab-Israeli peace negotiation, did not sit well with Rabin. (The recent decision to satisfy Israel's demand for recognition of Jerusalem as its capital has deepened Arab animus toward the United States.) The conflict between the Palestine Liberation Organization (PLO), which had gained ascendancy as the representative of the Palestinian people and was adamant about destroying Israel, and Tel Aviv's determination to have no dealings with the PLO, threw up an additional barrier to progress.

In April 1977, a visit to Washington by Egyptian president Anwar

Sadat "brightened prospects" for a Middle East settlement. He was a charming personality who exuded optimism at the same time that he held a bleak view of his country's future if he could not reach some kind of settlement with his Israeli neighbor. He also struck positive notes with Carter by expelling Soviet advisers and asking for U.S. military supplies to replace Soviet arms. But in May, when Menachem Begin, an ultraconservative leader of the Likud Party, became Israel's prime minister, hope for successful future negotiations all but disappeared. The tensions over Israel's 1967 conquests on the West Bank of the Jordan and the Golan Heights abutting Syria were taken off the table as negotiating chips—"land for peace"—in any future talks with Israel's Arab neighbors.

In November 1977, eager to advance Egyptian well-being, Sadat made known that, if invited, he would go to Jerusalem to meet with Begin to talk peace with Israel. When Sadat arrived in Israel on the nineteenth, he was greeted with appropriate fanfare and was invited to speak before the Knesset. His visit and speech offered Israel recognition and the normalization of relations. But major barriers to a new relationship remained to be negotiated. Sadat wanted Israel to give back to Egypt the Sinai, which Israel had occupied in the 1967 war. He also wanted Israel to vacate the left bank of the Jordan and reach an accommodation with the Palestinians. But Begin saw the West Bank as not only essential to Israel's security but also as part of its heritage. In December 1977, delegations meeting in Cairo immediately came up against insurmountable differences. As Stuart Eizenstat, who was part of these discussions on the American side, wrote later, "In negotiating domestic and international agreements . . . it is just as important to know your opponent's problems . . . as it is to know your own." Neither Begin nor Sadat had expanded their thinking to consider what the other man required to reach a settlement.

Carter stepped in to further the talks. In February 1978, he invited Sadat to join him at Camp David, to strategize about bringing the two sides together. In March, Begin came to Washington, where the president confronted him with the reality that a refusal to return occupied territories and to recognize the right of the Palestinians to some sort of self-government would doom the peace talks for years to come. Begin remained unyielding; the meeting was unpleasant for everyone and left Carter convinced that Begin lacked the vision to achieve peace. Though in April, when Carter announced the establishment of a commission to build a memorial museum in Washington to the victims of the Holocaust, it reduced some of their tensions.

Carter was so dogged in his determination to find common ground that he invited Begin and Sadat back to meet with him in September at Camp David. He hoped that the peaceful, bucolic setting would encourage an agreeable mood, despite almost two years of futile negotiations. His determination rested on his belief that they were the only three leaders who could do it, and that failure would mean additional intermittent Arab-Israeli wars that could involve the U.S. and USSR. Carter thought that in three days they would either reach an agreement or abandon the talks.

The negotiations, however, stretched out for thirteen days. To guard against public agitation during the discussions, the press was barred from daily reports on their progress. Because Begin and Sadat had little rapport between them (Sadat described Begin as "a very formal man, difficult to approach or understand"), Carter became the essential bridge between the two adversaries. He spent much of his time "defending each of the leaders to the other." The talks entailed a grueling back-and-forth that repeatedly threatened to collapse. They struggled with three great issues: Israeli occupation of the Sinai, Israel's continuing presence on the West Bank of the Jordan, and the status of the Palestinians. Control of Jerusalem also shadowed their discussions. When the conversations reached an impasse and the two leaders seemed about to break off the talks, Carter urged them not to leave the room and to let him try to find some middle ground for compromise between them.

Carter's patient mediation, which rested on an understanding that an agreement served both long-term Israeli and Egyptian interests as well as his political standing in the United States and abroad, paid off in a "Framework for Peace in the Middle East" and a "Framework for an Egyptian-Israeli Peace Treaty." The Camp David settlement of September 17, 1978, permanently—but not entirely—changed conditions in the Middle East and won Begin and Sadat a Nobel Peace Prize.

Carter came to the presidency against the backdrop of the Nixon-Kissinger initiative that had launched a new era in Sino-American relations. But existing ties to Taiwan blocked normal relations with Peking, where China's previous Nationalist rulers and Mao's foes had created an island fortress with U.S. financial and arms support. Normalization of Mao's government also jeopardized better relations with Moscow and the negotiation of a strategic arms limitation treaty. In particular, a mutual statement of Sino-American opposition to "hegemony," which was Chinese code for Soviet expansionism, angered Moscow. To quiet advocates of Taiwan's autonomy, which U.S. recognition of the mainland communist regime seemed to jeopardize, Carter supported a Taiwan Relations Act, which guaranteed protection to the island from a communist invasion and agreed to provide them with modern arms. At the same time, however, he recognized Peking as the only Chinese government and ended diplomatic recognition of Taiwan as China's government, though we continued to have a continuing relationship with the Taiwan regime.

By 1980, as Carter prepared to run for a second term, a host of problems stood in his way. The hostages remained in captivity in Iran. The economy was in poor shape, with wholesale prices increasing by 20 percent in the first quarter of the year and a large federal budget deficit that fueled inflation. Despite having Democratic majorities in both houses, Carter could not get a divided party to follow his lead on the economy. With the national debt at 32 percent of the gross domestic product (GDP), the Republicans were able to condemn Carter as a profligate manager of the national economy. With the national debt reaching 107 percent of the GDP in 2018 following a trillion-dollar tax cut by the Republicans, it is not difficult to understand why the White House and party, despite traditional complaints about deficits and debt, now have little, if anything, to say about the country's vastly expanded red ink.

A split in the Democratic party between conservatives and liberals opened up a contest for the presidential nomination in the spring and summer of 1980. Massachusetts senator Ted Kennedy, Jack and Bobby's younger brother, led the liberal challenge to Carter. Although Carter won enough delegates in his primary contests with Kennedy to assure himself of the nomination, the summer convention continued to demonstrate a "badly divided party." Even after Kennedy acknowledged Carter's nomination, his grudging appearance at the convention with Carter during his acceptance speech played badly on TV and, in Carter's assessment, seriously damaged Carter's re-election chances. As bad, Carter's national approval stood at only 20 percent. It was even worse than Nixon's low of 25 percent when he resigned. An influx of Cuban refugees fleeing Castro's control of the island added to the sense of a U.S. government unable to manage yet another problem.

The Republican Party's nomination of Ronald Reagan, the former governor of California, initially gave Carter hope of victory. Reagan's outspoken conservatism on domestic matters and belligerence toward the Soviet Union, suggesting an escalation of war dangers, seemed to give Carter an edge with centrists, whom Barry Goldwater's candidacy had frightened in 1964. Like Goldwater, Reagan spoke of voluntary Social Security, attacked welfare cheats, said Medicare would end freedom in America, opposed the progressive income tax as a form of socialism, and decried FDR's New Deal as destroying initiative and free enterprise. Nevertheless, with the burden of a questionable track record as president, Carter trailed Reagan, who despite his movie-star glamour came across to voters as an amiable, unpretentious man.

Carter and his advisers hoped to undermine Reagan in a nationally televised debate in Cleveland two days before the election. But a veteran television performer like Reagan understood that style and appearance, as it had favored Kennedy over Nixon in 1960, could give him an edge over Carter, even if Carter had a better grasp of the issues. True to form, Reagan used memorable one-liners to best Carter. When Carter attacked him for threatening to end Social Security and Medicare as we know them, Reagan distracted the audience with the dismissive "There you go again," as if Carter were a tiresome one-note candidate. And Reagan ended with a more subtle attack on Carter's presidency, asking voters, "Are you better off now than you were four years ago?" Many of the hundred million watching the debate discounted Carter's warnings about Reagan as a dangerous right-wing radical endangering welfare programs and international peace. They came away convinced that Reagan was a better alternative to an administration burdened by a stumbling economy and the unresolved hostage crisis. The Reagan campaign's acquisition, by stealth, of Carter's preparatory debate book may or may not have given Reagan an edge in preparation. But even without that dirty trick, it is unlikely that Carter would have found the means to throw Reagan on the defensive and win the debate.

Reagan won the election in lopsided fashion, taking forty-four of the fifty states. The result spoke volumes not just about Carter's failed record but also the extent to which personal appeal magnified through television helped carry the day.

However ignorant Reagan may have been about national and international problems, he grasped that an electorate influenced by TV images and advertising slogans were vulnerable to superficial public pronouncements regardless of their reliability. At the same time, Carter's term had deepened antagonism to politicians and anyone with a reputation for great intelligence. Reagan proved that the nearer they could present themselves as ordinary Americans, the more appealing they were to the average voter. Carter had a difficult time pretending to be anything other than what he was. Posturing is a surprising advantage in presiding over the Republic. And though Carter certainly deserves high marks for the Middle East advances in Israeli-Egyptian relations, his overall record makes him a second-rate president, at best. He left the economy in poor shape and did nothing to convince Americans that the Washington of Nixon had been cast aside by his term in office. His failure to bring the hostages home from Iran made him seem incompetent as a national security leader. He lost to a second-rate actor in his bid for a second term, and did nothing to convince voters that a highly intelligent politician is more desirable than a man of ordinary intellect with limited knowledge of the country's history.

CHAPTER 10

Ronald Reagan

The Media President

———

By 1980, the United States had become a mass entertainment society. Films, radio, and newspapers had been serving as vehicles of information and entertainment since the 1920s. Newspapers, of course, had kept the mass of Americans abreast of current events going back into the nineteenth century. But the limits of literacy had cramped the reach of print journalism into the twentieth century. Radio and film had greatly expanded this audience, but it wasn't until the 1950s, with the advent of television, that news and entertainment could reach into most homes every day. And with this came the triumph of celebrity. True, America had been hooked on the idea of popular heroes as early as the eighteenth century, with widespread admiration for George Washington and pioneers like Daniel Boone, and toward the close of the nineteenth century with the moguls of wealth like Andrew Carnegie, John D. Rockefeller, and J. P. Morgan. In the twentieth century, sports and film heroes like Babe Ruth and Jack Dempsey and Greta Garbo and Charlie Chaplin had all become household names.

But the appeal and reach of national celebrities only entered the political arena in the 1960s when George Murphy, a Hollywood song-and-dance star, won a California Senate seat and opened the way for Ronald Reagan, another Hollywood actor, to use his high public visibility on film and television to become a winning candidate for governor of California. True, John Kennedy had made TV a vehicle for turning a politician into a star, but first Murphy and then Reagan perfected the art. In the late 1960s Reagan's conservative message on excessive government intrusion with taxes, and its excesses on abortion and political correctness, found a large receptive audience. His counter to the anti-war, antireligious, public hedonism of the time helped elevate him to the governorship. He promoted himself as an ordinary American from a Midwest small town who had risen to fame in Hollywood by living the American dream of upward mobility.

This was not far from the truth, but it was hardly the full picture. Reagan brought with him to politics romantic Hollywood illusions about cure-alls and happy endings. George H. W. Bush called his central economic plan "voodoo economics," or what later became known as supply-side economics or Reaganomics. The idea that cutting taxes and government regulations would pay for itself has proved false time and again, with big tax cuts greatly increasing the federal debt.

As governor, Reagan promised to oppose a California withholding tax, and to oppose a woman's right to choose an abortion, but would ultimately prove to be more of a political realist than a conservative ideologue. When the state struggled with fiscal shortfalls, he did not hesitate to sign a withholding tax law. When journalists reminded him that he had said that his feet were in concrete on that issue, he replied with characteristic and disarming humor, "Gentlemen, the sound you hear is the concrete breaking about my feet." Similarly, when he decided to run for president and read national polls demonstrating that abortion rights enjoyed a national majority, he signed into law the most progressive state abortion statute in the nation.

In 1964, when Goldwater ran against Johnson, Reagan supported Goldwater with a televised message "A Time for Choosing," in which he denounced "a little intellectual elite in a far distant capital [who think they] can plan our lives for us better than we can plan them ourselves." He manifested no recollection of how Roosevelt's New Deal had rescued his father, an unemployed shoe salesman, from poverty with federal aid. He also echoed the complaints of "working men and women" who, he said, were forced to support welfare cheats too lazy to work and too ready to rely on government doles. How much he believed any of what he said was difficult to tell. He told Stuart Spencer, a public relations adviser, "Politics is just like show business. . . . You begin with a hell of an opening, you coast for a while, and you end with a hell of a closing." In short, never mind the content, it was razzle-dazzle that counted, and he soon gained a reputation as "The Great Communicator."

While Reagan ran for president in 1980 as a principled conservative who described the Soviet Union as an evil empire, his appeal largely rested on his public familiarity, eight years as California's governor, and as a clear alternative to Jimmy Carter's errant presidency. Most presidential elections seem like an opportunity for something better than what had transpired in the past four years. True, some sitting presidents have managed to convince voters that they are improving national affairs and deserve a second term, especially if the alternative seems less than exciting. But because only two Republicans—Eisenhower and Nixon, who did as much to expand government programs as eliminate them—had won the presidency since Roosevelt, it is not surprising that Reagan's rhetoric promised dramatic change or the "Reagan Revolution." The disappointments with Johnson and Vietnam, the collapse of honest government with Nixon and Watergate, Gerald Ford's unpopular presidential pardon, and Jimmy Carter's weakness in the hostage crisis and management of the economy made the thirst for heroic action a compelling part of Reagan's appeal. He had already played the part of American hero in films, and as Reagan's biographer Lou Cannon described it, Reagan was about to assume "the role of a lifetime."[1]

In 1981, when Reagan entered the presidency, he announced in his Inaugural Address that "government is not the solution to our problem. Government is the problem." He promised to put the country's financial house in order by reducing taxes (building on California's 1978 Proposition 13 that cut property taxes nearly in half, with support from two-thirds of the state's voters), protect the unborn, and restore religious truths to America's schools. And though Reagan would become known, thanks to the *New York Times*'s Tom Wicker, as "President Feelgood," the first two years of his term were anything but that.

In 1981–82, as the Federal Reserve moved to rein in 14 percent inflation by raising the federal funds rate to 20 percent, the country fell into the worst economic decline since the Great Depression. U.S. unemployment, which stood at 7.5 percent in May 1980, had jumped to 10.8 percent by November-December 1982, while Alabama, Michigan, and West Virginia each exceeded 14 percent joblessness, and bank failures reached heights not seen since the Depression. The human suffering had echoes of the misery of the thirties. Tent cities occupied by homeless Americans sprang up around the country and were called "Reagan ranches" instead of "Hoovervilles." More than eleven million people were unemployed in the 1980s downturn. Steel production, then a principal index of the nation's economy, fell to

35 percent of capacity. And Reagan's approval tumbled from 60 to 41 percent, reaching a low of 35 percent in January 1983, when a majority of Americans did not want him to run again for president.

Spurred by a Reagan tax cut in 1981 that reduced the highest bracket from 70 to 50 percent and the lowest from 14 to 11 percent and a concurrent arms buildup, the national debt jumped in 1980 from $908 billion at 32 percent of the country's GDP to $1.377 trillion at 37 percent of GDP in 1983. By 1989, the end of Reagan's two-term presidency, he had reduced the highest tax bracket to 28 percent, while the debt had reached $2.85 trillion at 50 percent of GDP, despite tax increases that took back much of the 1981 deductions that were largely offset by increased military spending.

However much the economy stumbled in 1981–82, it did not permanently alienate a majority of Americans from Reagan. They continued to see him as a soft-spoken, likeable man. But it wasn't just his persona that sold him to so many in the country; it was also his toughness in dealing with adversaries. They liked his blunt rhetoric about communist Russia, and loved it when in June 1987 he stood before the Brandenburg Gate in Berlin and said, "Mr. Gorbachev, open this gate! Mr. Gorbachev, tear down this wall," meaning, of course, the Berlin Wall that had divided East and West and penned in East Germans and Eastern Europeans under authoritarian rule.

As early as 1981, a majority of Americans had seen Reagan as "a strong leader." In March, he had not only survived an assassination attempt, but also had the presence to joke with the surgeons as they wheeled him into the operating room, "I hope you are all Republicans today." His humor under adversity amplified his toughness. In August, he scored again with the public when he fired over eleven thousand members of PATCO, the Professional Air Traffic Controllers Organization, who had struck for higher pay that disrupted air travel and threatened greater inflation. By expressing sympathy for the strikers as he dismissed them, he came across again as a nice man who was simply doing what he thought best for the nation. Columbia University economist Robert Lekachmen described the irony of "the nicest president who ever destroyed a union . . . and compelled families in need of public help to first dispose of household goods in excess of $1,000." In 1981, Paul Conrad, the *Los Angeles Times* cartoonist, depicted an urchin child in front of a tenement with her hand out and a stern Ronald Reagan telling her, "You don't look truly needy to me . . . needy perhaps but not truly needy!"

At the same time, Reagan warred with the media over its coverage of economic suffering, complaining especially about television that had done so much to make him a star and had carried him to the White House. Nevertheless, he was able to convince much of the country that the recession was not the product of what his administration or the Federal Reserve were doing, but the result of a profligate government that had been on a spending binge under Democratic presidents.

During the 1981–82 recession, Reagan's approval rating consistently stood below 50 percent, and most commentators thought he could not win again in 1984. Moreover, congressmen who dealt with him saw him as out of his depth on most policy issues. They would arrive in the Oval Office and Reagan would respond with an inane greeting. He often could not recall their names, which did not please either party's participants in these meetings. Reagan would read to them from four-by-six cards, demonstrating his dependence on aids to keep him abreast of the issues under discussion. On one occasion, Tip O'Neill, the Democratic House leader from Massachusetts, exploded in anger when Reagan resorted to his habit of telling an anecdote (this time about an unemployed worker who preferred the welfare dole to a job offering). "Don't give me that crap," O'Neill shouted at him. "Those stories may work on your rich friends, but they don't work on the rest of us. I'm sick and tired of your attitude, Mr. President. I thought you would have grown . . . in office, but you're still repeating those same simplistic explanations."

A Republican congressman at the meeting told the journalist Lou Cannon off the record, "Tip's right. The President's just out of it too much of the time." Clark Clifford, LBJ's secretary of defense, described Reagan as "an amiable dunce." Some in the administration thought Reagan was a "trusting dolt" who could be bent to any well-informed person's will or at least give the impression of someone open to changing his mind. In fact, Reagan was very stubborn and steadfastly held to fixed opinions.

But a majority of Americans didn't see him as a rigid and uncaring conservative, and refused to buy the Democrats' criticism of him as insensitive to the suffering of the unemployed and the needy. And so, in 1983–84, when the economy made a sharp comeback, the public was ready to give Reagan credit. Fed chairman Paul Volcker's easing of the money supply gave the economy the boost it needed. But even then it was not a robust recovery. As Lou Cannon pointed out, "The nation's private wealth grew only 8 percent in the six years after the end of the recession." Moreover, the national debt almost tripled, "the trade deficit more than quadrupled," and the United States became "a debtor nation for the first time since 1914."

Yet in 1984, the economic upswing gave Reagan talking points in his bid for a second term. As the economy improved, Reagan declared, "They aren't calling it Reaganomics anymore," which is what critics had dubbed the economy when it was faltering. That year, one of the knocks on Reagan was his age; at seventy-three, he appeared to be slowing down. His biographer Lou Cannon compiled a catalogue of gaffes: When he greeted Singapore prime minister Lee Kuan Yew to the White House, he said, "It gives me great pleasure to welcome Prime Minister Lee Kuan Yew and Mrs. Lee to Singapore." He called Los Angeles mayor Tom Bradley "Mayor Bartlett," and misspoke 1941 as 1981. He said, "We are trying to get unemployment to go up, and I think we are going to succeed." As confusing, he declared, "Even though there may be some misguided critics of what we're trying to do, I think we're on the wrong path." And he told some businessmen, "Nuclear war would be the greatest tragedy . . . ever experienced by mankind in the history of mankind." His incoherence was on full display when he advised some students heading to Europe, "It's all right to have an affinity for what was the mother country for all of us, because if a man takes a wife unto himself, he doesn't stop loving his mother because of that. But at the same time, we're all Americans." When he went to Bitburg, Germany, where he visited a cemetery with Nazi SS graves, it provoked angry criticism. It also provoked a joke at Reagan's expense: He thought he was visiting Pittsburgh.[2]

As usual, Reagan used humor to deflect questions about his age and competence. In 1984, during a debate with the fifty-six-year-old Walter Mondale, Carter's vice president and his Democratic opponent in the election, Reagan joked, "I will not make age an issue of this campaign. I am not going to exploit, for political purposes, my opponent's youth and inexperience." Even Mondale could not help laughing. All the back-and-forth between Reagan and Mondale over leadership, the economy, deficits, Social Security, Medicare, and other future policies faded alongside Reagan's quip. And it shielded him from further complaints about his advanced age and possible incompetence to serve another term.

In 1984 Reagan won one of the greatest landslides in American presidential history. Aided by the flourishing economy; Mondale's announcement that he would raise taxes to reduce the national debt; the continuing widespread affection for "the Gipper," as Reagan was dubbed for his role in the popular film biography of Notre Dame football coach Knute Rockne; the view that Reagan had unified the country; and two very skillful television ads, "The Bear in the Woods," touting Reagan's resistance to Soviet communism, and "Morning in America," an upbeat reminder of the good economy, Reagan captured forty-nine of the fifty states with 525 electoral votes and 58.8 percent of the popular vote. Only Minnesota, Mondale's home state, and D.C., a Democratic enclave, voted against him, giving Mondale a scant 13 electoral votes, despite having made New York congresswoman Geraldine Ferraro his running mate, the first woman in U.S. history to be a vice presidential nominee.

Reagan's second term from 1985–89, as with so many other second presidential terms, was less effective, though he continued to hold the affection of much of the public through the missteps of the next four years. But for all the support Reagan enjoyed, many Americans worried that his anti-communist rhetoric could provoke a war with the Soviet Union. He called on the West to conduct a "crusade for freedom," which was aimed against Moscow's control of Eastern Europe, and predicted that Marxism-Leninism would end on the "ash heap of history." His rhetoric came under attack as too strident and undermining peaceful resolutions of tensions with the Soviet Union. In March 1983, when he spoke to the National Association of Evangelicals and called Moscow "the focus of evil in the modern world," it frightened some Americans as challenging Russia to a showdown. At the same time, Reagan promoted a Strategic Defense Initiative (SDI) known better as "Star Wars," a delusional program promising military technology that would shield against ICBMs and mutually

assured destruction (MAD). The Soviets denounced Reagan's rhetoric as "irresponsible" and "insane." Reagan ran into additional overseas difficulties in the Middle East. When it came to foreign affairs in
his first term, Cannon asserts, "too often, Reagan was a performer
and presidential leadership was an empty shell." During foreign policy meetings with national security advisers, he kept his counsel—
largely because he was ignorant about the subjects under discussion.

Reagan often tried to settle an argument among his advisers by
taking a middle ground between them. In the contest between diplomacy and more aggressive action, Reagan usually favored a compromise. In the case of the Middle East in general and Lebanon in
particular, where a civil war had been raging since 1975, Reagan's
aggressive action "courted catastrophe." According to contemporary
analysis, it was "a case study of foreign policy calamity."

In June 1982, Israel, which initially enjoyed almost unqualified
support from Reagan, invaded Lebanon to suppress cross-border attacks by the Palestine Liberation Organization (PLO). In October
1981, Muslim extremists had assassinated Anwar Sadat in Cairo,
adding to instability in the region. His successor, Hosni Mubarak,
was eager to maintain Sadat's role of peacemaker, but events did not
cooperate. When Israel annexed the Golan Heights in December
1981, it further enflamed tensions between the Israelis and the Syr-
ians. An attempted assassination of the Israeli ambassador in London by a Muslim militant triggered the Israeli invasion of Lebanon to
suppress the PLO; it shortly became a full-scale attack that reached
Beirut. With the conflict in Lebanon producing terrible civilian casualties, Reagan agreed to send U.S. marines as part of an international
peacemaking force along with French and Italian troops. When calm
seemed to be returning to Lebanon after a few weeks, the coalition of
Western forces withdrew.

But within days, the assassination in Beirut of Lebanon's newly elected president, the Christian leader Bashir Gemayel, ushered in attacks by Gemayel's forces on Palestinian refugee camps, where they massacred seven hundred Palestinians, including women and children. In response, the U.S., France, and Italy returned their multinational force to Lebanon, though U.S. military chiefs were wary of a risky deployment in an unstable country. Within days of the return of U.S. marines to Beirut, a suicide bomber destroyed the U.S. embassy, killing seventeen Americans. The marines now became the targets of daily attacks. In the fall of 1983, as marines began to die in the fighting, it provoked memories of Vietnam, where the United States was caught in the middle of a civil war. And as with Vietnam, Reagan invoked the danger of expanded communist control, this time in the Middle East. Reagan declared that the United States could not "stand by and see the Middle East incorporated into the Soviet bloc." His knee-jerk anti-communism missed the reality that the Arab states were no more ready to accept Moscow's control than that of their former colonial masters.

Reagan also lost sight of the greater reality that hostile Muslim forces in Lebanon saw the United States as an ally of Israel and representative of the neocolonial West. They did not see the U.S. as a peacemaker but rather as a threat to their autonomy and an inviting target of terrorist operations. The U.S. chiefs pushed the idea of redeploying the marines to ships stationed offshore, where they would largely be out of harm's way. But Reagan, like Johnson before him, saw U.S. troops as invulnerable to some massive assault. Reagan was mistaken, and it cost the marines 241 lives when a suicide bomber drove an explosive-laden truck with twelve thousand tons of TNT through several barriers into a barracks where 350 men were sleeping on a Sunday morning; it was "the largest non-nuclear blast on record." Reagan, consumed by grief, justified the loss as in pursuit of "a noble cause," but was finally convinced to move the remaining marines over the next three months to ships offshore. Like Johnson's eroded popularity, Reagan's public standing fell.[3]

But not for long, because at the same time Reagan ordered an invasion of Grenada, a tiny island in the Caribbean that had a population under a hundred thousand in an area of 135 square miles. Suspicions abounded that the invasion, which came two days after the catastrophe in Lebanon, was as much a reaction to that as to conditions on the island. What ostensibly provoked the invasion was the turmoil of a Marxist government that threatened to become like Cuba, which had stationed some of its troops on the island. For Reagan, it meant that Grenada was likely to become another communist center for subversion in the Western Hemisphere. As much to the point, though, was the danger to eight hundred American students at the St. George's medical school on the island. In the invasion and subsequent fighting, it took two days for U.S. forces to subdue the Cubans, causing nineteen American military deaths and 845 defenders killed. But the successful invasion was solace of a kind for the losses in Lebanon. Reagan publicly linked the two as part of a broader U.S. resistance to communist aggression, and it worked to boost his public standing.

For a while, Reagan was adept at hiding his America First policy in Central America. Mindful of the divisions in the United States over Vietnam and how they had destroyed the Johnson presidency, Reagan was determined to mute his anti-communist actions in the region. He understood that anything resembling gunboat diplomacy would not only stimulate traditional anger against what Reagan called "the colossus of the North"—anti-American critics called us the "monster of the North"—but would also generate domestic opposition to his administration that could undermine his chances of

winning a second term. He was determined not to look like the policeman of the hemisphere regardless of how the U.S. acted behind
the scenes. But an unwise and unproductive intervention in Nicaragua's politics gave the lie to his cover-up.

In 1979, after the left-wing Sandinistas ousted the government
of Anastasio Somoza, a corrupt dictator, Carter provided financial
support to the new regime. But instability continued in Nicaragua,
as it also dogged an El Salvador torn between a pro-American government and leftist guerrillas. Reagan could not bear to see what he
thought would be communist advances so close to the United States.
"The Soviet Union underlies all the unrest that is going on," Reagan
said without mention of the many economic and social difficulties
that beset the region and of the perception that the U.S. was an architect of these troubles. He knew next to nothing about Central America. When he returned from a trip there, he said, "Well I learned a
lot. . . . You'd be surprised. They're all individual countries." But
he still couldn't let go of the single-minded assumption that Moscow
was the overarching problem he faced in the area. Ignoring Soviet
control of Central America would, in Reagan's mind, mean the loss
of America's worldwide credibility, the collapse of our alliances, and
jeopardy to the continental United States. It was a replay of the logic
that got us into Vietnam.

Reagan's solution was to counter communist influence with clandestine operations that would not make the front pages of the newspapers and become a source of domestic agitation, as had happened
with Vietnam. It was all a study in unthinking reductionism. The
CIA mined Nicaraguan harbors to prevent foreign arms shipments to
the government. Reagan called the contras battling the government
"freedom fighters" and approved CIA supplies to them, as well as air
and sea attacks against the Sandinistas. The "covert war," Cannon

asserted, ran for seven years, "cost thousands of lives and hundreds of millions of dollars, [helped] devastate the shaky Nicaraguan economy, bitterly divide the U.S. Congress, damage the reputation of the CIA, and undermine Reagan's capacity to govern."[4]

During closed-door discussions with advisers, Reagan would reveal the limits of his intellect and understanding, especially of foreign policy issues. He "was often so obviously wearied by extensive analysis . . . that aides plunged into arcane material at their peril. If Reagan became sufficiently bored, he simply nodded off." He preferred clear, simple explanations that more often than not he found in *Human Events,* a conservative publication that reduced matters to black and white, bad guys and heroes. It suited Reagan's affinity for moralistic pronouncements that could move him and an audience.

At the same time, Reagan had a genuine desire to promote national and international harmony. True, his second term would stumble through the Iran-contra crisis, but it was also especially notable for his commitment to improving Soviet-American relations, which First Lady Nancy Reagan had encouraged him to pursue. To be sure, conditions in the Soviet Union and the rise of Mikhail Gorbachev to the leadership of his country in 1985 made a world of difference in opening the way to better relations. But it needed both men with an understanding of the value of diminished tensions to reduce the dangers of a nuclear holocaust and advance détente.

In 1985, after Reagan began his second term in January, he was eager to find some common ground with Gorbachev, who had succeeded to Soviet leadership in March. The resumption of arms control talks in Geneva, Switzerland, was an initial step toward détente. Although these discussions would reach an impasse over U.S. insistence on preserving SDI, Reagan's favorite idea for assuring U.S. national security, it did not discourage him from inviting

Gorbachev to Washington. Reagan saw a summit conference as a chance for him and Gorbachev to get to know each other and move forward on their shared eagerness to reduce nuclear arms and threats to peaceful relations. Cordial exchanges of correspondence led to an initial summit meeting in Geneva in November 1985.

From the start, both men liked each other. Yet initially, they could not overcome the difficulties long provoked by suspicions of each other's intentions. When Reagan proposed to share his cherished SDI technology with Moscow to assure against a surprise attack, Gorbachev refused to believe it and predicted its development would cause an arms race in space. Similarly, when Gorbachev said that the Soviet Union had no aggressive intentions and that the U.S. was trying to bankrupt the Soviet economy, Reagan denied it and cited Soviet attempts to undermine democracies. Yet because they shared a desire for détente and prospects for immediate significant agreements seemed remote, they agreed to future summits in each other's capitals and put out a statement describing the Geneva meeting as successful in agreeing to mutual reductions in nuclear arms.[5]

In April 1986, an explosion at a nuclear reactor in Chernobyl, Ukraine, released radiation into the atmosphere that drifted as far as Japan, and created an additional incentive for Moscow and Washington to rein in the nuclear arms race. It "was less than one warhead and look what happened," Reagan said. It spurred the resumption of summit negotiations during two days in Reykjavik, Iceland, in October 1986, which would be a prelude to a more full meeting in Washington in 1987. The back-and-forth at the Iceland meeting led Gorbachev and Reagan to broach the possibility of eliminating all nuclear weapons. But their idealistic vision fell victim to Reagan's insistence on keeping his Strategic Defense Initiative, promising again to share any advances in developing a defense shield against nuclear weapons that would give both countries basic security or "a good insurance policy for both sides." In response, Gorbachev maintained his demand that SDI's development be confined to the laboratory and not be deployed even if it worked, which remained an open question. Reagan refused to abandon his dream of a nuclear safety net, which critics of the idea continued to mock as "Star Wars." The discussions broke up over this impasse.[6]

By December 1987, the two sides were ready to meet again in Washington. Gorbachev's commitment to "glasnost"—openness— and "perestroika"—economic reform—and a mutual treaty commitment to a reduction of intermediate- and short-range nuclear missiles in Europe (INF, for "intermediate-range nuclear forces") made him seem a new kind of Soviet leader who would decisively improve Soviet-American relations. On his arrival in Washington he was greeted like a hero. In public, he spoke about the need for changing the way both sides thought about each other. Apparently aware of how U.S. politicians campaigned, he mingled with crowds and enjoyed their shouts of approval. In a summit session they signed the INF treaty, the first agreement between them to reduce arsenals, and Reagan, ever mindful of lingering suspicions of communist tactics, declared the treaty was an expression of trust but would include provisos to verify it. Although it would require considerable arm-twisting by Reagan to overcome conservative opposition, the Senate approved the treaty as Reagan was about to go to Moscow for a reciprocal summit visit in May-June 1988.

The Moscow visit was of little substantive consequence, but it was symbolic of a new day in Soviet-American relations. Thoughts of a nuclear war between the two superpowers now, thankfully, seemed more than unlikely. In a reprise of what Gorbachev did in Washington, Reagan was like a man on the campaign trail in Moscow, drawing admirers who became unruly and moved the Soviet secret police, the KGB, to mount an attack on the surging crowd. By all accounts, they simply wanted to see or get close to the president. For Reagan, it seemed like confirmation that the Soviet Union was still a "police state." And Reagan took every opportunity to underscore his and America's regard for freedom—of speech, thought, religion, and all the other benefits that people enjoy in a democratic society. Although their summits did not entirely end the Cold War or signal the full collapse of Soviet imperialism, they decisively announced a new era in Soviet-American relations.[7]

The close of the Reagan presidency was not simply a triumph of foreign relations but also entailed a scandal that once more tested public faith in a president and the country's political institutions. Between 1982 and 1984, congressional resolutions prohibited support for Nicaragua's anti-Sandinista contra rebels. But administration officials, with or without an inattentive president who was described as having lost his focus at the age of seventy-three, cut a deal with the Iranian government to sell them antitank and antiaircraft missiles, despite Reagan promises not to collaborate with any terrorist regime, including Iran. The payments for these weapons were transferred to the contras in violation of the congressional limitations on aid. After the Democrats regained control of the Senate in the 1986 congressional elections, they launched joint House-Senate investigations into these Iran-contra dealings, which led to the appointment of a special counsel, Lawrence Walsh. He eventually charged fourteen people with criminal wrongdoing that led to the convictions of eleven administration officials, including Vice Admiral John Poindexter and Colonel Oliver North. Two convictions were overturned on appeal, and eight pardons by the subsequent George H. W. Bush administration shrank the punishments to a minimum.

The Reagan scandal cast a pall over his presidential legacy. But it did not shatter his hold on the public. In January 1983, at the depths of the recession, his approval had fallen to 35 percent. But in the midst of his second term, in January 1987, he reached a high of 71 percent approval. And despite the Iran-contra scandal, he left office with a 63 percent positive rating. The average of his approval rating during his eight-year presidency was 52.8 percent. Reagan's popularity carried over into the 1988 election. Although the House of Representatives remained under Democratic Party control throughout Reagan's eight years, he held the Senate for Republicans six of those years. Yet Reagan's popularity remained so strong that voters were ready to give him a third term; of course the Twenty-Second Amendment forbade more than two. The alternative that Reagan gave them was his vice president, George H. W. Bush, who had faithfully served under him for eight years, despite their harsh words about each other in their competition for the 1980 Republican nomination. In addition, no one could quarrel with Bush's qualifications for the higher office. He had served in World War II as a navy aviator, and for eight years as a Texas congressman; and been U.S. ambassador to the United Nations, chairman of the Republican National Committee, ambassador to China, and director of the CIA.

Even with such impressive credentials and Reagan's support, Bush did not appear to be a sure bet. No vice president had succeeded to the presidency since Martin Van Buren in 1836, and no party had won three presidential elections in a row since Truman and the Democrats in 1948. But scandals brought down the Democratic Party's two front-runners in 1988: Colorado senator Gary Hart by an extramarital affair and Massachusetts senator Ted Kennedy by Chappaquiddick—an accident in 1969 that cost the life of twenty-eight-year-old Mary Jo Kopechne and put Kennedy and the Democrats on the defensive. The party's candidate, Massachusetts governor Michael Dukakis, was a reasonable choice, but his campaign fell victim to Bush's attacks on him as a Northeast liberal who was soft on crime. The Bush campaign's "Willie Horton" ad that roasted Dukakis for favoring a Massachusetts furlough program that allowed convicts to leave prison for a weekend seriously undermined his candidacy. Crimes of rape and murder by Horton when on furlough pilloried Dukakis as weak on crime. Photos of Dukakis, who had no record of military service and tried to counter this by riding in a tank with a helmet that critics said made him look like Snoopy, backfired and embarrassed him. Seen as the heir to Reagan's legacy, Bush won a one-sided victory: Forty states to ten for Dukakis and an electoral margin of 426 to 111, as well as a seven million popular vote advantage.

George H. W. Bush's four-year term, followed by his defeat in his bid for a second term, fanned the ambitions not only of Bill Clinton, who defeated him, but also George W. Bush, who wished to revenge his father's loss, and Barack Obama, who accurately believed that he could win the presidency. Donald Trump saw Carter's stumbles, Bill Clinton's impeachment, George W. Bush's failed war in Iraq, and the unusual event of an African American president as providing the right moment for a political novice like himself to win the White House. Perhaps no one opened the way to Donald Trump's presidency more than Ronald Reagan. He demonstrated that a largely unsophisticated actor could capture the country's support in a presidential election and largely hold on to it through two terms, despite ups and downs in the economy and some stumbles in foreign affairs. Above all, Reagan demonstrated the appeal of a media personality in converting his popularity into political fame. Yet the Reagan experience should also be a cautionary lesson in the limits of someone with inadequate knowledge of history.

CHAPTER 11

Trump

In the Shadow of History

———

Every successful president has been seen as an inspiring visionary, a sort of prophet who leads the country into a new time of change and improvement. The most successful of our modern chiefs identified themselves with what was considered "new" and different: hence TR's New Nationalism, Wilson's New Freedom, FDR's New Deal, JFK's New Frontier, LBJ's Great Society, and Reagan's Revolution. Turning back the clock to normalcy, as Harding promised, or making America Great Again or Keep(ing) America Great, as Trump proposes, are more backward-looking than far-seeing and cannot win or sustain majority support for the long term.

All these pre-Trump administrations were pretty much a blank slate to him. Judging from what he has said about earlier administrations, it is difficult to believe that he knows much about them or, more generally, American history. It was only with the Bill Clinton, George W. Bush, and Barack Obama presidencies between 1993 and 2017 that he saw vulnerabilities he hoped to exploit to become president. Yet there were traditions in place going back to Theodore

Roosevelt at the start of the twentieth century that made Trump's ascent to the presidency and behavior in office possible. The behaviors that Trump replicated were largely kept from contemporary public view. Only later in most instances did we learn about them, like presidential health problems, involvements abroad, womanizing, or secret dealings with Iran.

Trump has believed that his slogan, "Make America Great Again," is enough to persuade Americans of a president's ability to lead the country. But presidents who promised a brave new world or a journey on to new frontiers understood that it was essential to move beyond slogans or compelling bumper stickers; they gave substantive meaning to their words. TR's use of the government to mediate differences between labor and management; his assertion of federal authority to assure the purity of drugs and food; his use of presidential power to police the trusts or business conglomerates of the time, including the railroads that had become the leaders of modern transportation and exploited their workers; and his interventions abroad that promoted an image of America as a proponent of international commerce serving all mankind, and a peace arbiter among backward-looking nations at war, promised a better day. It all elevated TR to a place among history's greatest presidents—Washington, Jefferson, Madison, Monroe, Jackson, and above all Lincoln. From the perspective of more than a hundred years later, TR remains a leading light among all the nation's chiefs.

Woodrow Wilson does not stand far behind. His New Freedom is enshrined in history as a further step forward in making the federal government a promoter and defender of democratic principles. Building on TR's domestic advances, his presidency introduced additional domestic reforms to benefit women and children, management of the national economy through a Federal Reserve Bank, and additions to popular rights through constitutional amendments: the graduated income tax (Sixteenth), the direct election of senators (Seventeenth), and women's right to vote (Nineteenth). His greatest and in many ways most popular and least successful appeal was to make democracy the world's principal governing system and eliminate international conflicts with a League of Nations. It's true the latter never fully came to pass, though the League gave life to the United Nations and Wilson's dreams made him one of the world's great political visionaries.

No modern president did more to transform national and international politics than Franklin Roosevelt. Promising to make his generation of Americans "prophets of a new order," his New Deal with its many social programs that established the welfare state, humanizing the country's industrial system, and his leadership in overcoming isolationism to defeat fascism, Nazism, and Japanese militarism and in turning the United States into the world's premier power overseeing what the publicist Henry Luce called the American Century, established Roosevelt, along with Washington and Lincoln, as one of the three greatest presidents in American history. Seventy-five years after his death, FDR's idealism and pragmatism remain a model for aspirants to the White House who see government as a benefactor to peoples everywhere.

Harry Truman also left an indelible mark on the United States by concluding World War II with the atomic bombings of Japan and completing FDR's transformation of foreign policy from isolationism to internationalism. Truman's containment policy to counter Soviet communism has secured his place in the front rank of presidents: the Truman Doctrine providing economic aid to Greece and Turkey that blunted Soviet subversion in the Near East; the Marshall Plan that rehabilitated Western Europe and preserved its democratic governments; and the North Atlantic Treaty Organization (NATO), the first defensive-offensive alliance in American history. Truman's unpopularity at the end of his term in 1953, spawned by the stalemate in Korea, has morphed into his standing as a great president who won the Cold War, or at least set the country on the path to victory in the Cold War, through his skillful and tough-minded policies. And Truman's 1948 upset election victory over Thomas Dewey also stands as an unmatched mark in presidential history.

Dwight Eisenhower is also a memorable president. Although Republicans have elevated Ronald Reagan to the position Ike formerly held as the party's leading modern president, he continues to stand as a successful leader of the nation and the Republican Party. While he confirmed FDR's welfare state as a permanent part of the nation's domestic life by expanding some New Deal measures, he fell short on foreseeing the national shift on black civil rights. His greatest achievements were in ending the Korean fighting and in advancing Truman's containment policy blunting Soviet aggression. And though he initiated the actions that trapped us in Vietnam, he brought the country through eight years in the fifties with no major international conflict. In addition, he presided over an administration that suffered no major scandal, and managed to win two White House terms for his party.

John F. Kennedy is now also remembered as a visionary leader who not only established the Peace Corps and put Medicare, federal aid to education, and civil rights at the center of American politics, but led the United States into the space age. His promise to put a man on the moon by the end of the sixties assured his presidency of retrospective greatness when it occurred in 1969. It gave meaning to what he meant when he called his administration the New Frontier. His test ban treaty reining in nuclear explosions that poisoned the atmosphere now has even greater meaning when the world is more mindful than ever of how human destruction of the environment is threatening future generations on planet Earth. Those currently fighting for environmental protections would do well to remind people of Kennedy's test ban. His determination to prevent a nuclear war with the Soviet Union that could have permanently devastated the planet resonates now as much as it did in the 1960s when he saw the importance of détente with Moscow.

Lyndon Johnson's 207 legislative achievements also had transformative consequences for the United States. His completion of JFK's agenda on Medicare and education helped improve life for Americans of all ages, as did his many laws protecting the environment and consumers. None, however, made a greater difference in serving the national well-being than the 1964 Civil Rights and 1965 Voting Rights statutes. Both laws gave meaning to fundamental American promises of equal treatment for all citizens, but also demonstrated the country's capacity for growth and improvement from the dark days of slavery and Jim Crow bias that limited the horizons for people of color. Johnson's 1965 immigration reform that overturned the 1924 National Origins statute, which he called "racist," established more humane requirements for access to the United States. (What a contrast his record and language about immigrants and immigration is with what Trump says and does.) Johnson's vision of a Great Society and a war on poverty faltered alongside the Vietnam War that cast a permanent shadow across his presidency. Still, his many domestic achievements remain as a demonstration of a president who saw a realistic path to a better America.

Ronald Reagan's eight-year presidency is no match for any of his Democratic predecessors in domestic affairs, and his snide observation that we fought a war on poverty and poverty won does him no credit as a visionary leader. Yet he holds high ground in following

JFK's legacy of working to rein in and end the Cold War. Reagan was fortunate in having a youthful visionary partner in Russia's Mikhail Gorbachev, who shared Reagan's desire to reduce and even eliminate the possibility of a nuclear conflict between the two superpowers that could permanently devastate the earth. While Truman's containment policy was the foundation of keeping the Cold War from turning into a human holocaust, Reagan's receptivity to shifting away from seeing Moscow as an "evil empire" to a cooperative nation determined to preserve life on earth as we know it deserves recognition. He became a president with a vision of a better global future.

In the third year of his presidency, Donald Trump said that no president had accomplished more than he did in his first two and a half years in office. His statement is nonsense. For one, it is hard to think of Donald Trump as a visionary president in any way. Making America great again hardly satisfies any standard for leading us into a better future. True, during his administration the economy has enjoyed a time of low unemployment and general prosperity that Obama had put in place, but it is difficult to see just how Trump's economic policies have advanced the country's economic well-being. Yes, his $1.5 trillion tax cut has served corporations and the wealthiest Americans and buoyed the economy for a time, but it has done little for less affluent citizens. And if and when the next recession hits the United States, the Trump economy will enjoy little standing as a landmark moment in U.S. economic history and will be remembered for running up the national debt when its tax cut did not generate a promised reduction in the country's red ink. Nor will his presidency as of 2020 be seen as anything but a retrograde force in international affairs. Despite Trump's rhetoric about great advances, there has been no groundbreaking in relations with North Korea or Russia, or in the Arab-Israeli conflict, only adding to Middle East tensions by moving the U.S. embassy from Tel Aviv to Jerusalem and legitimizing Israel's settlement of the West Bank territory occupied since the 1967 war.

Modern America has seen the rise of celebrity presidents. Beginning with Theodore Roosevelt and the advent of the penny press, chief executives have enjoyed special national and international fame. No president who hoped to achieve greatness could do it by only enacting laws. Men like Calvin Coolidge and Herbert Hoover were portrayed in the press as dour characters whom few in America were eager to follow. Both Theodore and Franklin Roosevelt impressed their personas on millions of citizens as models of what Americans should admire and imitate, and now stand as exemplary presidents.

TR gave initial meaning to the role of president as a celebrity whose family life and heroic actions set a standard every American could admire. Reporters gave Roosevelt an outlet for promoting himself as the embodiment of what a modern president should be and do. TR's accomplishments at home and abroad excited men and women across party lines and made the country proud of a larger-than-life national and international figure who made America the envy of the world. However little most Americans know now about someone who served in the White House more than a hundred years ago, the name Theodore Roosevelt continues to have positive reverberations.

Part of TR's appeal rests on the reputation of his cousin Franklin. No president since TR at the start of the twentieth century captured the public's imagination more successfully than FDR. His masterful use of radio with his fireside chats on Sunday evenings brought him into people's homes as a welcome guest, and his long tenure in the White House made him seem indispensable. After he died in 1945, a man stood sobbing by the railway track as the train carrying the president's body back to Hyde Park for burial passed by. Someone asked the mourner if he knew the president. "No," the man replied, "but he knew me." It was a telling expression of how Roosevelt had impressed himself on the citizenry. Similarly, after FDR died, a woman stopped Eleanor Roosevelt on the street and said, "I miss the way your husband used to talk to me about my government." People thought of him as a president who did all in his power to improve their lives.

Few Americans believed that anyone, let alone Harry Truman, the "little man from Missouri," could possibly fill FDR's shoes. But Truman was no slouch as a politician. He understood that he needed to create his own role in the American political drama. When he stood up to the Soviets to contain their aggression, it made him a new American hero. But nothing captured the public's approval more than his 1948 run for president as an underdog candidate. His whistle-stop train tour with his blunt language about the "do-nothing, good-for-nothing" Republican Congress moved crowds to yell, "Give 'em hell Harry." He made an indelible impression on voters as someone who had emerged from Roosevelt's shadow and deserved support in his own right. Although his popularity largely collapsed for a time, few forgot his fighting style, and he would eventually be elevated in the public's mind to standing as a great president.

No president after FDR, however, managed to sustain a hold on the public's imagination during his time in office more successfully than Dwight D. Eisenhower. The campaign button stating "I Like Ike" said it all. It was not his presidential accomplishments in domestic and foreign affairs that made an indelible impression on the average American. Rather, it was the man who enjoyed the public's affection as a war hero in leading the country to victory in World War II and ending the Korean War. But it was also the glow of his persona, with his warm smile and down-to-earth manner, that captured the public's affection. True, Ike fell short in recognizing that ending racial segregation was essential to national advancement, though he did not hesitate to enforce court mandates of school integration in Little Rock, Arkansas.

John F. Kennedy, his successor, was able in the course of his thousand days in the White House to make himself into another national hero. His assassination at the age of forty-six, with the promise of his presidency unfulfilled, made him an unforgettable American martyr. But Kennedy was more than a martyr; he had some substantial accomplishments, like the Cuban missile crisis that avoided an unprecedented nuclear war and the test ban treaty. It is not strictly these actions, however, that fasten him so much on people's memories. He was the handsomest man to ever sit in the White House, and television made him into a kind of Hollywood star. The combination of glamour and tragedy that marked his life and that of his family became an unforgettable part of JFK's legacy.

For all of Lyndon Johnson's brilliance as a legislator with an unmatched record of success except for FDR, LBJ never commanded the public's affection as the two Roosevelts and Kennedy did. He was seen as an overbearing and unlikeable personality, with vulgar qualities that offended ordinary Americans. Humor about a president is telling in defining the public's attitude toward him. Two stories about Johnson say it all: He stopped his car while driving about his ranch in Texas and stepped out to urinate on the ground. When one of his Secret Service escorts, who was guarding him, complained that Johnson was urinating on his leg, Johnson supposedly replied, "I know, son. That's my prerogative." The story about Johnson displaying his penis in response to a reporter's question about Vietnam added to his crude image. Whether either of these stories is true is not the point: The fact that they were used to make fun of Johnson speaks volumes about public impressions of him and have affected his reputation as a successful president.

Trump's constant drumbeat of attacks on critics in abusive language bothers millions of Americans who believe a president's use of language should preserve the dignity of the office. Until Trump, every president understood that no one serves in the White House without coming under public attack. Unlike Trump, they understood that being president meant exposure to public criticism and best countered it with humor, and by doing so endeared themselves to the public, showing themselves to be above the hurly-burly of political warfare. Ronald Reagan is a good example of a president who deployed humor to disarm his critics. It will stand as a Reagan hallmark, as Trump's lack of humor and his coarse, degrading language will dog Trump's postpresidential reputation.

The advantage of all these presidents who used their engaging qualities to bring the public, and voters especially, to their sides should not be discounted or diminished alongside their other attributes in leading the country. The contrast of presidents like TR, Wilson, FDR, Truman, Eisenhower, Kennedy, and Reagan to Donald Trump is compelling. Trump's appeal as an aggressive, combative, but successful business mogul was and remains important in explaining his hold on millions of Americans. But it has its limits. His name-calling of anyone who voices even the slightest criticism of him offends millions of other Americans who see him as a heavy-handed boor. His attack on FBI agents as "scum" in December 2019 for failing to support his claims of Ukrainian rather than Russian interference in the 2016 campaign is a telling example of his crudeness. At the end of the day, people find much to admire in a president who knows his mind and asserts himself, especially against other foreign leaders who seem to be in competition with the United States. But oral sex with her in the White House all the more damning. Trump is making a record as a remarkable presidential liar. In an October 28, 2019, story on the front page of the *New York Times*, after U.S. Special Forces had killed Abu Bakr al-Baghdadi, the leader of the Islamic State, Trump described him as "whimpering and crying and screaming" before he blew himself up in a tunnel, where he was trapped. The commanders of the operation said they had no idea what Trump was talking about. Others in the Defense Department dismissed Trump's description as an invention of his imagination.

As destructive to a president's hold on the popular imagination is their failure to deliver on what they promise. Woodrow Wilson suffered an unrecoverable setback when he could not fulfill his promises to make the world safe for democracy, with a war that cost Americans over fifty thousand battlefield lives, the war to end all wars. In the last months of his term, Wilson was a defeated president not only because his illness immobilized him but also because he had disappointed hopes of a brave new world. FDR's unqualified promise at the close of his 1940 third-term campaign not to involve the country in the war undermined his credibility when the attack on Pearl Harbor forced us into the conflict. His promise opened him to the sort of attack the historian Charles C. Tansill leveled against him in a 1946 book, *Back Door to War*, as having deceived the country about keeping the peace. Lyndon Johnson's repeated promises of victory in Vietnam would become mocked as the "credibility gap." No president since Johnson, Nixon, or Clinton has had so much tension with journalists and the press about lying than Trump. Complaints abound that he lies about everything: his extramarital affairs, wealth, abilities, accomplishments, and the results of his polices; a drained Washington political swamp; a wall on the southern border paid for by Mexico; a nuclear-free Korean peninsula; a peace agreement for the Middle

East; a new health care plan with significantly lower drug costs; a tax cut benefiting everyone; a reduced federal debt; and a massive program of new roads, bridges, tunnels, hospitals, schools, and airports paid for by an economic expansion funded by the tax cuts. His accusations against Robert Mueller, Adam Schiff, Nancy Pelosi, and other Democrats in Congress, and anyone else investigating him and others in his administration as witch hunters making up false charges have no more credibility than anything else he says. Trump has established himself as the least trustworthy occupant of the Oval Office since Richard Nixon, and as a president with a shrinking base of supporters. Unlike Nixon, who won in a landslide in 1972 and whom 25 percent of the public continued to support even after he resigned, Trump has never enjoyed majority backing, and his record of fabrications has made any larger popular appeal unlikely.

Trump's presidency has also fallen short in creating anything resembling a consensus in the country. The greatest presidents have been masterful in promoting agreement over the variety of differences across regions, races, religions, and ethnicities in the United States. FDR's New Deal scored a triumph of sorts when it overcame the split between urban and rural America and moved forty-six of the forty-eight states to back him in the 1936 election. Roosevelt's ability to win an unprecedented four terms described a country that had come together as at no time since the Era of Good Feelings in the early nineteenth century. Harry Truman's skill in creating a Cold War consensus to meet the Soviet threat was no simple challenge in a nation with a long history of isolationist bias against involvements abroad. Eisenhower, Kennedy, and Johnson for a time skillfully presided over popular majorities, as did Reagan, who turned many Democratic voters into Reagan Republicans. Subsequent presidents like George H. W. Bush, Gerald Ford, and Jimmy Carter saw the challenges of maintaining national support as a mountain peak out of reach.

The skill all presidential consensus builders found essential was the sort of pragmatic political shifting about that all successful presidents since TR demonstrated. Wilson won his domestic advances by appropriating Theodore's New Nationalism. A cartoon describing Wilson sneaking away with TR's clothes while he was in a swimming hole said it all. When Herbert Hoover called Franklin Roosevelt "a chameleon on plaid" in the 1932 campaign, he foresaw FDR's affinity for political flexibility, including his decision to make Henry Stimson and Frank Knox, both Republicans, members of his war cabinet. Roosevelt described himself as like a quarterback on a football team who tried to find plays that worked. Truman also relied on pragmatic politics to maintain public backing. Despite his antagonism to Republican critics shouting about subversives in the government, for example, he sponsored a loyalty oath requirement for all federal employees. He was not defending the country and government from subversives as much as he was meeting conservative demands for tougher action against subversion.

John Kennedy, after his close-run election against Nixon, imitated FDR when he appointed Robert McNamara and McGeorge Bundy, both Republicans, to major jobs in his administration. Johnson, who was a great admirer of FDR, made a career of moving across political lines, first as a senator and then as president. Typical of Johnson, he told a reporter who asked why he had recently said kind things about Richard Nixon after years of negative remarks, "Son, you need to understand that in politics, overnight chicken shit can turn to chicken salad." Johnson never saw a bill he couldn't arrange to pass by reaching agreement with congressmen and senators who demanded changes. Reagan had skills comparable to his pragmatic predecessors. As governor, he abandoned his opposition to withholding tax when it became essential to balance the state budget, and signed the state's liberal abortion statute when he saw it as helpful in running for president. He abandoned his talk of Soviet Russia as an "evil empire" when he saw a flexible negotiating partner in Gorbachev who could work with him to reduce, if not eliminate, Cold War tensions.

Donald Trump has been an unreliable negotiator in his dealings with Congress. Legislators have learned to distrust what he says he will support in a bill. In discussions with advocates of reform laws, Trump has shown initial flexibility but has rarely followed through on what he promised. His interest, for example, in reaching an agreement on a measure helping "dreamers" realize hopes of permanently staying in the United States has fallen short of any constructive result.

Trump has repeatedly proved to be something other than a traditional president of the United States. It's fine if you are aiming to bring about constructive actions to the office. But Trump seems more like a rebel without a cause, or someone who is in opposition to accepted norms without any positive program or results. And by the end of 2019, his unorthodox behavior as president had led to his impeachment for abuse of power and obstruction of Congress. His Senate trial generated acrimony that deepened the divide in the country between Trump's supporters and opponents. On a Senate vote to summon witnesses that seemed certain to further condemn Trump, the Senate split, 51 Republicans opposed to 49 in favor: 45 Democrats, two independents, and two Republicans. Most of the Republicans supporting Trump accepted an argument from retired Harvard law professor Alan Dershowitz that a president running for reelection in the belief that he will be best at serving the national interest is immune from impeachment and removal from office; at best, a questionable assertion.

In the February 10, 2020 *New Yorker*, Amy Davidson Sorkin called it "a pseudo-intellectual scaffold for Trump's self-delusion." On February 5, 2020, on Impeachment Article One, 52 Republican senators voted to acquit Trump, while all 47 Democrats and one Republican, Mitt Romney, voted "guilty," 20 votes short of a conviction. Article Two won the backing of all 53 Republicans, with the 47 Democrats voting "yes." Sorkin predicted that Trump "will undoubtedly see an acquittal as further license for abuse." It began the next day when he took a victory lap before Republican members of Congress and the press with a verbal assault on his critics, including a broadside against Romney. Although he denounced the impeachment as a "hoax" perpetrated by his Democratic opponents in the House, it is clear that he had brought this on himself by pressing Ukraine's new president to investigate former vice president Joe Biden, whom Trump saw as his likely opponent in the 2020 election.

The question future historians will want to ponder about Trump is not only how earlier presidents opened his way to the White House, but whether there is something deeper in American society that spawned so unsuitable a character to become president, or was it just a fluke and will recede or disappear in the next election with a return to more traditional candidates and a president who behaves in more familiar ways? In June 2019, *New York Times* and *Washington Post* reporters and columnists probed the underlying currents that brought so unsuitable a man to the presidency. While neither could provide persuasive answers to the question of just why our politics have fallen into this slough of despond, they have challenged all of us to wonder how we got here, and whether in the face of this unsettling moment in American history our democracy is reaching an untimely end, or we are just passing through another one of our episodic downturns that have unsettled our democratic Republic before.

Acknowledgments

Decades of reading, teaching, and writing about recent United States history and especially about twentieth-century presidents form an essential background to the composition of this book.

As with every book I published, the assistance of others has been invaluable.

John Wright, my literary agent, facilitated my writing and publication by HarperCollins. Conversations with Peter Kovler helped shape my conclusions about Donald Trump. Rebecca Dallek and Mike Bender came up with the title. Geri Dallek, Matthew Dallek, Michal Kazin, David Kennedy, and Richard Weiss read the manuscript and provided constructive suggestions for revision of construction and content.

I am indebted to Jonathan Jao for encouragement and editing of the manuscript that has made this a more readable book. Sarah Haugen, the associate editor, skillfully managed the work of converting the manuscript into a book. The copy editor, Josh Karpf, did an excellent job of eliminating errors and improving my prose. Any errors that remain are entirely my responsibility. I would add to this that my critical assessment of Trump as a president and politician are the result of his behavior, and future commentators on his term as president will more than likely view him as lacking the background and temperament to serve as an effective leader.

Notes

EPIGRAPH
1. John Dos Passos, *The Ground We Stand On* (1941).

INTRODUCTION
1. Thomas Jefferson, Inaugural Address, 1801.
2. Richard Rovere, *Senator Joe McCarthy* (1959).
3. Richard Hofstadter, *The American Political Tradition and the Men Who Made It* (1948), xxxvi.
4. Gerald Ford, Inaugural Address, August 9, 1974.
5. FDR speech, June 27, 1936.

CHAPTER 1 Theodore Roosevelt: "Master Therapist of the Middle Classes"
1. David Kamp, "Whether True or False, a Real Stretch," *New York Times*, December 30, 2008.
2. Ibid, 306; William E. Leuchtenburg, *The American President: From Teddy Roosevelt to Bill Clinton*, 36, 38–39.
3. Leuchtenburg, 52–53; Hofstadter, 275–78 and 306–7; H. W. Brands, *T.R.: The Last Romantic*, chapter 13, especially pp. 356–57, also 505–6.
4. Hofstadter, 291–95, 297–99; Leuchtenburg, 47, 59; Brands, 507, 512–13, and 517–18, chapter 21, especially pp. 541–42.
5. Leuchtenburg, 47–48.
6. Brands, 471–73 and 476–77.
7. *Ibid.*, 466–71.
8. *Ibid.*, 482–88.
9. Leuchtenburg, 67–68.
10. Brands.
11. See Brands, 528–40; and "Milestones in U.S. Foreign Relations: TR and the Russo-Japanese War," Office of the Historian, U.S. Department of State.
12. Brands, 578–83 and 605–16.

CHAPTER 2 Woodrow Wilson: Triumph and Tragedy
1. Brands, 309–10; John Milton Cooper, Jr., *Woodrow Wilson: A Biography*, 133.
2. Cooper, 73 and 182; and Hofstadter, 318–19.
3. Cooper, chapter 3, p. 58 for the quote; H. W. Brands, *Woodrow Wilson*, chapter 1,

pp. 17–18 for the quote. And the final quote is in Patricia O'Toole, *The Moralist: Woodrow Wilson and the World He Made*, 41.
4. On Harding, see Cooper, chapter 6, p. 488.
5. *Ibid.*, 128; O'Toole, 45.
6. Cooper, 187; Hofstadter, 331–37.
7. Arthur S. Link, *Woodrow Wilson and the Progressive Era*, 93.
8. Hofstadter, 351–67.
9. O'Toole, 425–32, 446, and 448.
10. Dean, 74.

CHAPTER 3 **Franklin D. Roosevelt: Prophet of a New Order**
Much of this chapter rests on my two FDR books: *Franklin D. Roosevelt and American Foreign Policy, 1932–1945* (1995 edition), and *Franklin D. Roosevelt: A Political Life* (2017); and my *American Style of Foreign Policy: Cultural Politics and Foreign Affairs* (1983), especially chapter 5.
1. George H. Gallup, *The Gallup Poll, 1935–1948*, see the polls for 1937 and 1938.
2. Eric Rauchway, "Great American Actor," *Times Literary Supplement*, April 27, 2018.
3. T. Harry Williams, *Huey Long*.

CHAPTER 4 **Harry S. Truman: The Tribulations of a Great President**
1. On Truman's vice presidency, see David McCullough, *Truman*, chapters 7 and 8, especially 327–28, 320, 339, and 342. Also, Robert Dallek, *Harry S. Truman*, chapter 2.
2. On the opening of the Truman presidency, see McCullough, chapters 9 and 10.
3. *Gallup Poll*, I, 512, 521–23, 527, 537, 557, 564–65, 567–68, 573, 581–82, 584, 587–88, 590–91, 594, 604, 606, 613, and 617.
4. McCullough, 586–89; *Gallup Poll*, 722.
5. *Gallup Poll*, 628, 632, 636, 640, and 661.
6. *Ibid.*, 727, 735, 739, 744–45, and 759.
7. The election is fully covered in McCullough, chapter 14.
8. On the hydrogen bomb, McCullough, 756–58; Truman's Inaugural Address is available online. The Acheson quote is in McCullough, 755. For the rest, see Dallek, *The American Style of Foreign Policy*, chapter 6.
9. McCullough, 887–94 and 903–14.
10. See Wikipedia for presidential rankings that, of course, include Truman.

CHAPTER 5 **Dwight D. Eisenhower: The General as Peacemaker**
1. *Washington Post*, February 22, 2019. Tom Wicker, *Dwight D. Eisenhower*, chapter 1; the quotes are from pp. 1, 8, 10, and 17.
2. Stephen E. Ambrose, *Eisenhower: The President*, 20–24, 116, 160, 201, and 253.
3. *Ibid.*, 24, 48, 115, 158, and 299–301.
4. Associated Press, "Text of Gen. Eisenhower's Wheeling Address," *St. Louis Globe-Democrat*, September 25, 1952, 6A.
5. Ambrose, 460. Jean Edward Smith, *Eisenhower in War and Peace*, 50–51, 53, 651–54, and 707. "National System of Interstate and Defense Highways," Wikipedia.
6. *Gallup Poll*, 1119, 1251, 1401–2, 1507, 1567, 1572–73, and 1724. Peter Lyon, *Eisenhower: Portrait of the Hero*, 409; Wicker, 96; Smith, 715–26.
7. Wicker, 27–28; Lyon, 469–70 and 534–35; Smith, 557–61 and 573–77.
8. Wicker, 23–24 and 81–82.

9. Smith, 617–27.

10. Lyon, 588–92 and 607–14.

11. Smith, 607–16.

12. George C. Herring, *America's Longest War: The United States and Vietnam, 1950–1975*, chapter 2.

13. Blanche Wiesen Cook, *The Declassified Eisenhower: A Startling Appraisal of the Eisenhower Presidency*, 158–61. Also see Jeff Broadwater, "Eisenhower and the Anti-Communist Crusade," and William Bragg Ewald, Jr., "Who Killed McCarthy?" in Michael S. Mayer, ed., *The Eisenhower Presidency and the 1950s*. The best argument for Ike's part in bringing down McCarthy is in David A. Nichols, *Ike and McCarthy: Dwight Eisenhower's Secret Campaign against Joseph McCarthy* (2017).

14. Smith, chapter 25, "Suez."

15. Lyon, 753–58; Smith, 743–46.

16. Smith, 746–51; *Gallup Poll*, 1586, 1596, 1617, and 1627.

17. Lyon, 809–15; Smith, 752–55.

18. Lester Langley, *The United States and the Caribbean in the Twentieth Century*, 212–18; Julia E. Sweig, *Cuba: What Everyone Needs to Know*, 74–79; Ambrose, 615.

19. *Gallup Poll*, 1699–1701.

CHAPTER 6 **John F. Kennedy: The Making of an Icon**

This chapter is largely based on my book *An Unfinished Life: John F. Kennedy, 1917–1963*.

CHAPTER 7 **Lyndon B. Johnson: Flawed Giant**

This narrative is largely drawn from my two volumes on LBJ, *Lone Star Rising* (1991) and *Flawed Giant* (1998).

CHAPTER 8 **Richard M. Nixon: America in Crisis**

This chapter is largely based on my book *Nixon and Kissinger: Partners in Power* (2007) and John A. Farrell, *Richard Nixon: The Life* (2017).

1. The best up-to-date narrative of the scandal is in Farrell, *Nixon*.

CHAPTER 9 **Jimmy Carter: The Moralist as Politician**

The principal sources for this chapter are Jimmy Carter, *Keeping Faith: Memoirs of a President* (1982) and Stuart E. Eizenstat, *President Carter: The White House Years* (2018).

1. *New York Times*, October 3, 2018.

2. On LBJ and nuclear weapons in Vietnam, see Michael Beschloss, *Presidents of War* (2018).

3. Gary Sick, "The Election Story of the Decade," *New York Times*, April 15, 1991; Neil A. Lewis, "House Inquiry Finds No Evidence of Deal on Hostages in 1980," *New York Times*, January 13, 1993.

CHAPTER 10 **Ronald Reagan: The Media President**

1. See Jill Lepore, *These Truths: A History of the United States* (2018), 624–27; Lou Cannon, *President Reagan: The Role of a Lifetime* (2000).

2. Cannon, 234–36, 332, and 438–40.

3. *Ibid.*, 339–90; see especially pp. 339–40, 343, 350–51, 365, 383, 386, and 389.

4. Walter LaFeber, *Inevitable Revolutions: The United States in Central America* (1984), 284–317.

5. The best book on Gorbachev is William Taubman, *Gorbachev: His Life and Times* (2017); Cannon, 666–77.
6. Cannon, 671–80, 685–92.
7. *Ibid.*, 695–710.

CHAPTER 11 **Trump: In the Shadow of History**
1. *Orlando Sentinel*, June 18, 2019.

Bibliography

Ambrose, Stephen E. *Eisenhower: The President.* New York: Simon & Schuster, 1984.

Beschloss, Michael. *Presidents of War: The Epic Story, From 1807 to Modern Times.* New York: Random House, 2018.

Brands, H. W. *T.R.: The Last Romantic.* New York: Basic Books, 1997.

Cannon, Lou. *President Reagan: The Role of a Lifetime.* New York: Public Affairs, 2000.

Cook, Blanche Wiesen. *The Declassified Eisenhower: A Startling Appraisal of the Eisenhower Presidency.* New York: Penguin Books, 1984.

Cooper, John Milton, Jr. *Woodrow Wilson: A Biography.* New York: Alfred A. Knopf, 2009.

Dallek, Robert. *The American Style of Foreign Policy: Cultural Politics and Foreign Affairs.* New York: Alfred A. Knopf, 1984.

———. *Harry S. Truman.* New York: Times Books, 2008.

Dos Passos, John. *The Ground We Stand On.* New York: Harcourt, Brace & Co., 1941.

Farrell, John A. *Richard Nixon: The Life.* New York: Doubleday, 2017.

Gallup, George H. *The Gallup Poll, 1935–1971.* 3 vols. New York: Random House, 1972.

Herring, George C. *America's Longest War: The United States and Vietnam, 1950–1975.* New York: Wiley, 1979.

Hofstadter, Richard. *The American Political Tradition and the Men Who Made It.* New York: Alfred A. Knopf, 1948.

LaFeber, Walter. *Inevitable Revolutions: The United States in Central America.* New York: W.W. Norton, 1984.

Langley, Lester. *The United States and the Caribbean in the Twentieth Century.* Athens: University of Georgia Press, 1982.

Lee, Bandy (ed.). *The Dangerous Case of Donald Trump.* New York: St. Martin's Press, 2017.

Lepore, Jill. *These Truths: A History of the United States.* New York: W.W. Norton, 2018.

Leuchtenburg, William E. *The American President: From Teddy Roosevelt to Bill Clinton.* New York: Oxford University Press, 2015.

Link, Arthur S. *Woodrow Wilson and the Progressive Era, 1910–1917.* New York: Harper & Row, 1954.

Lyon, Peter. *Eisenhower: Portrait of the Hero.* Boston: Little, Brown, 1984.

Mayer, Michael S., (ed.). *The Eisenhower Presidency and the 1950s.* Boston: Houghton Mifflin, 1998.

McCullough, David. *Truman*. New York: Simon & Schuster, 1992.

Nichols, David A. *Ike and McCarthy: Dwight Eisenhower's Secret Campaign against Joseph McCarthy*. New York: Simon & Schuster, 2017.

O'Toole, Patricia. *The Moralist: Woodrow Wilson and the World He Made*. New York: Simon & Schuster, 2018.

Rovere, Richard. *Senator Joe McCarthy*. New York: Meridian Books, 1959.

Smith, Jean Edward. *Eisenhower in War and Peace*. New York: Random House, 2012.

Sweig, Julia E. *Cuba: What Everyone Needs to Know*. New York: Oxford University Press, 2009.

Taubman, William. *Gorbachev: His Life and Times*. New York: W.W. Norton, 2017.

Wicker, Tom. *Dwight D. Eisenhower*. New York: Times Books, 2002.

Williams, T. Harry. *Huey Long*. New York: Alfred A. Knopf, 1969.

Index